Penny Warner

Kids' Party Games and Activities

Hundreds of Exciting Things to Do at Parties for Kids 2-12

Illustrated by Kathy Rogers

Meadowbrook Press
Distributed by Simon & Schuster
New York

Library of Congress Cataloging-in-Publication Data

Warner, Penny
    Kids' party games and activities/by Penny Warner; illustrated by Kathy Rogers.
       p.   cm.
    1. Games.   2. Amusements.   3. Children's parties.   I. Rogers, Kathy. II. Title.
    GV1203.W33   1993
    793'.01922—dc20   92-41900
                                                CIP

Publisher's ISBN: 0-88166-199-6

Simon & Schuster Ordering # 0-671-86779-2

©1993 by Penny Warner

Editor: Elizabeth H. Weiss
Production Coordinator: Matthew Thurber
Desktop Publishing Coordinator: Jon C. Wright
Designer: Tabor Harlow
Illustrator: Kathy Rogers

Published by Meadowbrook Press, 5451 Smetana Drive, Minnetonka, MN 55343

BOOK TRADE DISTRIBUTION by Simon & Schuster, a division of Simon and Schuster, Inc., 1230 Avenue of the Americas, New York, NY 10020

00 99 98   12 11 10

Printed in the United States of America

DEDICATION

To Tom, Matt, and Rebecca, who still love to play games.

ACKNOWLEDGMENTS

There were many parents and teachers who generously contributed their favorite games to this book. Many thanks to Kelly Ball, Linda Barde, Edith Bassett, Kirstin Branton, Cathy Bray, Heather Buchanan, Trude Evans, Christine Hunter, Jill Johnson, Michele Kane, Terry Kelly, Bruce Lansky, Jim Bohen, Marianne Mendonsa, Tawna Redick, Julie Roberts, Heather Thorton, and Doreen Warner. A special thanks to Elizabeth Weiss and Jay Johnson.

CONTENTS

PRETEEN 10–12

INTRODUCTION

IT'S PARTY TIME!

Whether it's a birthday party, a club meeting, or a classroom event, you want to have the best party ever. You've planned the theme, sent the invitations, and bought the goodies. The party room will be decorated, the cake will be a masterpiece, and the crowd will gather for a fun-filled event.

It sounds great. But how do you guarantee a terrific time for all? And what do you do between the time the kids arrive and the time they go home?

The answer is simple: plan plenty of games and activities to keep the kids entertained and delighted. And it's easy, with the help of *Kids' Party Games and Activities.* This book contains hundreds of exciting things to do during any children's gathering. The games and activities are appropriate for ages 2–12, the instructions are clear and simple, and the preparation is inexpensive and easy.

The book is divided into three major age groups, with each section containing a wide range of age-appropriate activities. The Preschool section (ages 2–5) offers easy-to-learn and easy-to-master games and activities for children who are gaining better control of their bodies and acquiring stronger language skills. The School Age section (ages 6–9) contains lots of physical and mental challenges for children who are skilled at both fine and gross motor activities and who enjoy races, puzzles, and creative fun. The Preteen section (ages 10–12) has games and activities that are more sophisticated for kids leaving childhood and entering adolescence. You'll find that many of these games can be enjoyed by kids older and/or younger than the age range specified. You know the guests best—read over some of the selections and decide what your group can handle.

Within each of the book's three major sections you'll find five types of party activities, including traditional games, contemporary games, group activities, outings and events, and entertainers. Whether you choose timeless favorites, new classics, or creative events, plan ahead! If you choose games that are too simple, the crowd will get bored. If the activities are too difficult, the kids might get frustrated, fight, or cry. If it rains during your outdoor games, the kids will be disappointed, and if they are cooped up inside too long, they'll wear you down. And if you don't have enough for the kids to do at the party, *everyone* will watch the clock in despair. Remember, be prepared, creative, and ready for anything, then approach the event with humor and patience. That way the party will be fun for you, your child, and the excited throng of guests.

How do you decide what types of activities to plan? It's easy! Just decide how much time you have for preparation and how many materials you want to buy, then let your child help you choose the games, activities, or events. And always have a contingency plan! For example, if you choose to have a stay-at-home party, pick a variety of indoor and outdoor games, active and quiet games, and competitive and noncompetitive games. If a game doesn't seem to be working, abandon it and go on to another—memorize the instructions so you don't have to consult the directions during each game. Group activities are fun for a creative crowd and work best

with lots of supervision and parental help. Entertainers provide a fun show-and-tell celebration and can make it easier on you, if entertaining a group of children isn't up your alley. Or take the kids on a party outing for an exciting, fun-filled day.

PARTY HINTS

These helpful tips will ensure a successful time:

- Choose a theme for the party. Ask your child what he or she would like as a focal point for the event and decorate around that theme. Perhaps a favorite toy, a special movie, or an often-watched TV show would make a good theme, complete with food, favors, and fun to match.

- Let your child help with the party planning. Find out what your child wants to do, and plan the event around that theme. If it's something outrageous, such as "go to Disneyland," suggest alternatives that incorporate his or her ideas and match your budget (such as a "Mickey Mouse Party," with a cake, decorations, and activities to match).

- Think the party through. Plan your time—two hours in the afternoon is best—and try to imagine how long each part of the party will

take: the welcome, games and activities, opening of presents, cake and ice cream, and good-byes. Let the guests' parents know when the party ends so you won't have to entertain beyond a set time.

- Invite your child's good friends and try to keep the group manageable. You don't have to invite everyone your child has ever met to the party. But then again, you may have to include an entire class at a classroom event. In either case, have a few parents on hand to help keep the event under control.

- Hire a babysitter to help during the party if you can't round up adult volunteers. Helpers will be invaluable during game time. They can work with kids who have difficulties with the activities, supervise play while you lead the game or decide the winners, and watch the kids while you prepare the food.

- Plan to have both quiet and active games to balance the kids' energy levels. Start out with a quiet introduction game, if the kids don't know each other, then let them release all that party energy with an active game or two. Then settle down again with a quiet game. When you're finished playing, have cake and open presents.

- Over-plan the games. A party can turn to chaos if there aren't enough games and activities planned, so be sure to have a few alternatives if the games run short.

- Tie in the games and activities to the party theme by renaming the games or using props to complement the theme.

- Have prizes for both the winners and losers, and don't place too much emphasis on winning. Pre-schoolers don't need competitive games and might get upset if they have to leave the game because of a mistake. Preteens, however, usually enjoy competition. School-age kids fall somewhere in between, so use your own best judgment when choosing games.

- Keep the sweets to a minimum and provide some healthy snacks, so the kids don't get too strung out on sugar. This will help keep the games under control, too.

- Let the weather be your guide. Make sure your activities can be adapted to indoor or outdoor play, if necessary.

- Keep the cameras handy (both video and still cameras) so you have a record of all the fun. If possible, take Polaroid snapshots to hand out to the guests as they leave.

- Expect problems—and roll with them. Be prepared to make adjustments if the kids don't enjoy a game or have trouble following the game's rules. Adapt to fit the needs of your guests, and change the rules to please the group. The goal is to have fun!

I hope the ideas in this book will help you plan a wonderful party for your child. May your event be a success!

Penny Warner

Preschool 2–5

DUCK DUCK GOOSE

Duck Duck Goose is a game that's popular with preschoolers because it's easy to learn and packed with lots of action and suspense.

For Ages: 2–5

Optional Ages: 6–9

Players Needed: 5 or more

Object: To get to the safety zone without getting tagged

HOW TO PLAY

All of the players sit cross-legged in a wide circle—they are the Ducks. Pick one child to be the Fox. The Fox walks slowly around the outside of the circle, tapping the top of each Duck's head lightly while saying "Duck" with each tap. After a few moments of this, the Fox chooses a Goose by tapping one player's head and calling out, "Goose!" The Goose must quickly rise and chase the Fox around the circle, trying to tag him before he reaches the spot where the Goose was sitting. If the Fox reaches the spot and sits down before being tagged, he is safe, and the Goose becomes the Fox. If the Fox is tagged while running, he must start the game again. Play continues until everyone has played the part of the Goose and the Fox or until the players are too tired to play anymore.

CREATIVE OPTIONS

• Change the Duck, Goose, and Fox to other animals or pets. The characters can be more contemporary—choose three characters from "Duck Tales," "Teenage Mutant Ninja Turtles," or *The Little Mermaid.*

• Make a simple tail from fake fur or construction paper and attach it to a belt for the Fox.

• Make the game more complicated for older children by having the Fox say the name of each player as he goes by and then call out the *wrong* name to signal the chase.

• Another variation is to play Duck Duck Gray Duck, with the kids saying "Gray Duck" to signal the chase. For added fun, they can put other adjectives in front of the word "Duck" as they go around the circle. For instance, a child could say, "Red Duck," "Sleepy Duck,"

Materials Needed:
• Enough space for the players to sit in a wide circle and two players to run around it

"Silly Duck," and then say, "Gray Duck," to signal the chase.

PRIZES AND FAVORS

• Give each Fox who returns to the circle without getting tagged a small rubber duck or duck sticker.

• When the game is over, give everyone an animal sticker or small stuffed animal.

• Give all of the players a treat bag. Fill them with wrapped hard candies, jelly beans, M&Ms, or cookies and label the bags "Duck Chow." Or fill the bags with tasty crackers and label the bags "Quackers."

TROUBLE-SHOOTING TIPS

• Play this game outside, if possible. That way no one will bump into any furniture and get hurt.

• If the game must be played indoors, make sure it's played on a carpeted area. Linoleum can be slippery, and carpeting provides a softer surface if anyone falls.

• Draw pictures of ducks (or have the kids do it) and use the drawings to mark the circle. Sometimes during the chase, the Fox and Goose get confused about where the safety zone is. A picture, or even a piece of paper marked with an "X," can help eliminate confusion.

• Encourage the Fox to tap (rather than slap) the Goose's head or to just tap the person's back or shoulder—players can get carried away by the excitement of the upcoming chase and become careless!

PIN THE TAIL ON THE DONKEY

Pin the Tail on the Donkey is a classic for preschool party-goers—you can make it even more fun with a few creative updates. It's a good indoor game that's appropriate for a small or large group.

For Ages: 2–5

Optional Ages: 6–9

Players Needed: 3 or more

Object: To "pin" the missing tail back on the donkey

HOW TO PLAY

Before the game, tape a poster of a donkey to the wall of the party room (make sure the area in front of the poster is clear of furniture). Prepare a tail for each player by writing her name on the tail she'll use. This will prevent confusion over who wins.

At game time, have the players form a line in front of the donkey poster. One by one, hand them a donkey tail, blindfold them, and spin them in a circle three times until they are facing the donkey again. (When you blindfold children, make sure the blindfold isn't too tight and that it covers their eyes completely.) They must stick the tail where it belongs on the donkey—the player who gets closest to the correct spot on the poster is the winner.

CREATIVE OPTIONS

• Use a different animal poster—try a rabbit and have the kids stick a cotton ball onto the poster for the tail. You can find animal posters at any poster shop and at some card and stationery stores, or draw your own.

• Draw a funny monster shape on a large sheet of paper and have each child pin a different body part to it (such as an eyeball, mouth, foot, or hoof) to create a creepy-looking creature. You can cut out these body parts from construction paper for a colorful effect.

• Cut tails out of fabric or felt and let the kids decorate them before the game with glitter, paint, and other art materials. The kids can also draw the tails and/or help draw the picture of the animal.

Materials Needed:

- A wall
- A large picture of a tailless donkey and a donkey tail for each player (available at party supply stores, or draw your own donkey and tails)
- A blindfold, bandanna, large scarf, or eye mask with the peepholes covered with black construction paper
- Tape

PRIZES AND FAVORS

- Blindfold the guest of honor, spin her around three times, and have her place a small goody bag on each guest (pin the goody bag on the indicated spot yourself to prevent anyone from getting pricked). The goody bags will probably end up on the guest's sleeve, collar, belt loop, or another funny place!

- The homemade decorated tails make nice mementos of the party.

- Offer prizes and favors related to the game—for example, a donkey stuffed animal, like Eeyore, or horse stickers.

- Give each child a small poster to take home.

TROUBLE-SHOOTING TIP

- If a child is reluctant to wear a blindfold, let her be the last one to take a turn so she can see it's not too threatening. If she still refuses, allow her to play with her eyes closed.

TREASURE HUNT

Pirates aren't the only ones who love to look for treasure—kids do, too. A treasure hunt is a wonderful activity for any type of party, and best of all, everyone gets to take a bit of treasure home.

For Ages: 2–5

Optional Ages: 6–9

Players Needed: 4 or more

Object: To find the most hidden treasure in a set period of time

HOW TO PLAY

Before the guests arrive, hide the treats and toys all around the party room. (It's best to play this game before any others because the kids might inadvertently discover some of the treasure while playing other games.) Hide the items in plain sight by matching the colors or shapes of the objects with the objects in the party room. For instance, if you're hiding a red jelly bean, put it next to a red book on the shelf so it's camouflaged but still easy to find. Hide the items *behind* or *beside* furniture or other objects instead of inside drawers or between seat cushions.

At game time, gather the kids together, hand them lunch bags to hold the treasure, and tell them to find the hidden goodies. Give them three minutes (or more or less time, depending on the group) to find the items. Every time they find a toy or treat, they should put it in their

sack and quickly move on. When the time is up, count the items in each child's bag and see who found the most—that child is the winner.

CREATIVE OPTIONS

• Rather than having the kids keep what treasure they find, you can keep hiding the items and play again and again. Use recyclable items such as plastic Easter eggs, shells, or colorful beads instead of candy so the kids won't be tempted to snack between rounds. After each round give the player who finds the most items a prize.

• Let the kids take turns hiding all the treasure— it's fun for them to watch the rest of the gang try to discover their creative hiding places.

• Instead of letting the treasure hunt be a free-for-all, write up some cryptic clues to lead the kids from one site to the next (it's best for younger kids to work as a team). If you've

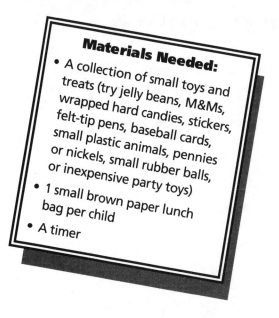

Materials Needed:
- A collection of small toys and treats (try jelly beans, M&Ms, wrapped hard candies, stickers, felt-tip pens, baseball cards, small plastic animals, pennies or nickels, small rubber balls, or inexpensive party toys)
- 1 small brown paper lunch bag per child
- A timer

hidden treasure in the bathtub, write a clue that says: "Rub-a-Dub-Dub," and let the kids try to figure out where to go next to find the reward. You'll need to read the clues to pre-schoolers or use pictures of objects cut out of magazines for clues, and you may have to coach them if they get stuck. Have a big prize waiting for them in one spot, such as a collection of goody bags, one for each child, or a bag of mini candy bars for everyone.

PRIZES AND FAVORS

- Let the kids keep the treasure they find.

- Give the kids bags of "pirate treasure" (gold-foil-wrapped chocolate coins tied with ribbon).

- If you use plastic Easter egg shells, fill them with goodies and give everyone a "goody shell" to take home.

TROUBLE-SHOOTING TIPS

- Make sure the treasure is hidden in plain sight and is no higher than preschoolers' eye level, so the kids can see and reach the items easily. If the kids are older, you can make the hiding places more obscure, but if they have trouble finding the items, give them hints such as, "Read any good books lately?" if you have an item hidden on the bookshelf.

- Let the kids know which areas are off limits so they won't wander to different places and waste their time.

- If one of the players doesn't find *anything*, hide a couple of trinkets in plain view when the rest of the kids are occupied with their own treasure hunting and give him a little help.

HOT POTATO

Hot Potato is a game that will really keep things "moving" at your preschooler's party. You can play indoors or outdoors—it's the perfect game for a large, energetic group.

For Ages: 2–5

Optional Ages: 6–9

Players Needed: 5 or more

Object: To catch and toss the Hot Potato quickly without getting caught holding it

HOW TO PLAY

The players sit cross-legged in a circle, facing the leader who is seated in the middle. The leader (you or one of the kids) starts the game by throwing the Hot Potato to a player of her choice, and then closes her eyes once the game gets underway (she must close her eyes so she can't tell who has the potato at any given time). The first player must catch the Hot Potato and toss it to another player quickly. Play continues with the Hot Potato getting tossed at random throughout the circle. If the Hot Potato is tossed out of play, the last person who touched it should be the one to fetch it.

After a short period of time, the leader shouts out, "Hot!" Whomever is caught holding the Hot Potato at that moment leaves the circle and is out of the game. The game continues in this manner with the players gradually being eliminated. The last player left is the winner.

CREATIVE OPTIONS

• If the game is played outdoors, use a water balloon for the Hot Potato so that the kids must handle it more gently—if it's dropped during play, it will break and splash water on everyone, adding an element of suspense to the game! Just be sure to tell the guests to bring bathing suits or old clothes to the party if you choose this game option. (To make a water balloon, stretch the opening of a de-flated balloon and attach it to a faucet. Holding the bottom of the balloon, turn on the faucet and slowly fill the balloon with water. Turn off the water, take the balloon off the faucet, and tie it closed.)

• Have the players toss hollowed, confetti-filled eggshells. Carefully poke two holes on either

Materials Needed:
- Enough space for the players to form a wide circle
- A potato, tennis ball, stuffed sock, beanbag, or water balloon

end of an egg and clean out the yolk by holding the egg upright and blowing through one hole. The yolk will drip out of the other hole—you might need to use a pin or needle to break up the yolk if it won't come out. Then rinse the eggshell with water and let it dry thoroughly. Once it's dry, use a funnel to fill it with confetti, tape both holes closed, and give it to the kids to toss back and forth—until the unexpected happens!

- Make a beanbag out of glittery or neon fabric and tell the kids they're tossing "hot lava" from a volcano. You can use different fabrics and your imagination to create other untouchable items, such as "pond slime" or "gopher guts"—the more disgusting the better!

PRIZES AND FAVORS

- If you're making a "hot" beanbag for the kids to toss, sew some extras for everyone.

- Make confetti-filled eggshells for each guest.

- Offer the grand prize winner a Mr. Potato Head kit.

TROUBLE-SHOOTING TIPS

- If you're worried about the kids randomly tossing the Hot Potato, have them pass it quickly around the circle one by one instead.

- Some players might get upset about having to sit out of the game because they got caught with the Hot Potato, so you can plan to play the game without having a winner. Kids who get caught with the Hot Potato can also take a turn as the leader. They will enjoy the pace of the game more than the competition.

- If you're using water balloons and some of the kids don't want to get wet, provide raincoats or plastic garbage bags for them to wear.

RED LIGHT, GREEN LIGHT

The suspense of Red Light, Green Light has made it a favorite for years. It's best to play this game outdoors in an open area, but it's possible to play indoors—if you have lots of space!

For Ages: 2–5

Optional Ages: 6–9

Players Needed: 3 or more

Object: To be the first one to tag the Police Officer without getting caught

HOW TO PLAY

Before the game, draw two parallel chalk lines or lay two ropes a good distance apart on the play area. Make sure there is plenty of space for the kids to run around between the chalk lines or ropes (twenty feet is a good minimum distance). Choose one player to be the Police Officer and have him stand in front of one line. All of the other players stand behind the opposite line.

The game starts with the Police Officer facing the other players. He turns his back to the other players and yells, "Green light!" Then he counts to five out loud as quickly as he can. The other players must run or walk quickly toward the Police Officer while he counts. When the Police Officer has counted to five, he shouts, "Red light!" and the players must freeze instantly.

The Police Officer whirls around to catch any players who are moving. Anyone who moves must return to the starting line. Play continues until one of the players crosses the line while the Police Officer's back is turned. That player then becomes the Police Officer.

CREATIVE OPTIONS

- Provide the kids with a special prop, such as a hat, shirt, or jacket when it's their turn to be the Police Officer. This makes it seem a little more official. A plastic "police" whistle is a fun prop, and the kids can use it instead of shouting the stop and go commands (give one to each child to prevent spreading germs).

- Have the Police Officer wave a scarf (or other light material item) in the air to make the other players move and drop it down when he wants everyone to freeze. This version is good

Materials Needed:
- A large playing area
- Chalk or 2 long lengths of rope

when the game is being played indoors because it's a little quieter.

- Make the kids do something silly when they get caught by the Police Officer such as hop, zoom like a car, or make animal sounds as they're going back to the line.

PRIZES AND FAVORS

- Let the kids keep their whistles or other props after they've been the Police Officer.

- Offer each player a book or coloring book about traffic signs, or make some homemade stop signs from red construction paper for the kids to play with at home.

- Pass out small red and green flashlights.

TROUBLE-SHOOTING TIPS

- Make sure that everyone gets a turn to be the Police Officer. If a player wins twice, have him pick another player so everyone has a chance to lead the group.

- Supervise the game to see that everyone plays fair. Some kids will cross the line at all costs and may need a little extra guidance so they don't gang up on the Police Officer.

- Choose a play area that's clear so the kids won't trip over the rope or run into anything.

MUSICAL CHAIRS

Kids love the classic game of Musical Chairs because it's full of excitement. You'll love it because it's a great way for a group of kids to let off some steam without getting out of control. Try some creative options if the kids don't want to stop playing!

For Ages: 2–5

Optional Ages: 6–9

Players Needed: 4 or more

Object: To be the last player in a chair when the music stops

HOW TO PLAY

Arrange the chairs in a line with every other chair facing in the opposite direction. If there isn't much space available, put the chairs back to back or in a circle. The players stand by the chairs, all facing the same direction.

Choose one player to be the leader, or play the leader yourself. The leader stands away from the players and is in charge of the music. When the leader starts the music, the kids march around the chairs in single file. As soon as the leader stops the music, the players scramble for the nearest empty chair and sit down quickly. Whomever is left without a chair leaves the game. One chair is then removed from the line so that there is one less chair than players. The game continues until two players are left to battle over one chair. The player who sits down first (when the music stops) is the winner.

CREATIVE OPTIONS

• Instead of chairs, use pillows or sofa cushions.

• Play music the kids will like, such as tunes from "Sesame Street" or the music of popular children's folk singers. Or prerecord a variety of songs, spaced at ten-second intervals, so no one has to monitor the music. You can also spin the radio dial and have the kids scramble for chairs when you get to a song.

• Tape an inflated balloon to the seat of each chair before the game and tell the players that they not only have to sit in the chair but also pop the balloon! This should prevent any disputes over who is actually sitting in the chair (the one sitting on top of the popped balloon gets to stay in the game). After each round, tape another inflated balloon to each chair. The kids will love the sound effects!

Materials Needed:
- Chairs for all but one player
- A cassette player and musical tape, or a radio

- For a really different version, toss items of clothing on the floor and spread them out so each piece is visible. Have one less item than players. Then use the basic rules of Musical Chairs to play, with the kids putting on a piece of clothing quickly when they hear the music stop. The player who doesn't get an article of clothing to put on is out of the game. Remove one item every time a player leaves the group.

PRIZES AND FAVORS

- Give each player a noisemaker or kazoo.

- If you play the clothing version of the game, purchase some special hats or inexpensive T-shirts that everyone can wear home.

- Give the kids cassette tapes featuring popular children's artists.

TROUBLE-SHOOTING TIPS

- When setting up, place the chairs about six inches apart to avoid a pile-up each time the music stops.

- If arguments over who's really sitting in the chair occur, repeat the round—this will prevent hurt feelings.

- Provide the kids who are out of the game with a small toy or treat so they won't feel bad about losing. Or let each one take a turn monitoring the music.

- Make sure the music is loud enough so everyone can hear it clearly.

SNATCH!

Kids love to be sneaky, and this game gives them a chance to be crafty—without getting into trouble. What's special about this game is that it's designed not to have a winner, so there's no direct competition between the kids!

For Ages: 2–5

Optional Ages: 6–9

Players Needed: 6 or more

Object: To secretly snatch an item from the party table

HOW TO PLAY

While the guests are in another room, place the objects on the party table (arrange them any way you want). Make sure the kids don't get to see what's on the table until you're ready to start the game.

The kids are to sit at the table, take a good look at the small items, and remember what they are. A chosen player then turns his back and closes his eyes. While his eyes are closed, point to another player and have this player quietly sneak one of the toys or treats off the table and put it in his lap, hidden from view. The first player can then face the group again—he must determine which item is missing from the table, and who snatched it. Allow him a few guesses and then have the culprit confess and show the stolen item. Return the item to the table before beginning the next round. The player who snatched the item leads the next round, closing his eyes and facing away from the group. Select another player to snatch an item. Play continues until everyone has had a chance to snatch and guess.

CREATIVE OPTIONS

- If it's too difficult for the kids to guess the snatcher *and* the missing item, just have the kids try to identify the snatcher. After every wrong guess, have the guesser close his eyes again while the snatcher sneaks another item. Continue to allow guesses until the culprit, with a lap full of goodies, is identified.

- While the guesser has his eyes closed, have the snatcher give him something personal instead of taking something away from the table. The player could take off a shoe or sock and set it in front of the guesser's place. The guesser must identify who the shoe or sock belongs to—without looking under the table!

Materials Needed:
- A table
- A variety of small, fun items, such as candy or tiny toys—1 item per player

- If the players are older, place lots of items on the table to make identifying the missing item more difficult. In addition to the small toys and treats, you could fill up the space with a cake, paper plates, cups, or napkins.

PRIZES AND FAVORS

- Let each player take home a toy or treat from the party table. If you don't want the kids to grab for items at the same time, tell them you'll pick a number from one to twenty and whomever chooses the correct number can pick an item first. (The player who is closest to the number is the second to pick an item, etc.)

- Play a final round where the prizes are hidden away in different-colored goody bags. As each player snatches a bag, let him keep the goodies inside once he has been identified. Place the empty bag back on the table for the next player's guess.

TROUBLE-SHOOTING TIPS

- Sometimes kids get so excited, they almost give away the "thief" by their body language. They can't help turning their heads toward the culprit, glancing at him several times, or even pointing. (Sometimes the "thief" even gives himself away by giggling!) Warn the players about being too obvious *before* the game, and it might help control their impulses a little.

- If younger players have trouble identifying the item taken from the table, just omit that part of the game. The real fun is trying to find the culprit!

COPY CAT

Kids love to copy each other, until they drive themselves (and everyone else) crazy! If you're looking for an indoor game that's quiet (except for the giggling), try Copy Cat.

For Ages: 2–5

Optional Ages: 6–9

Players Needed: 6 or more

Object: To imitate an increasing number of body movements

HOW TO PLAY

All of the kids sit in a circle so they can see each other clearly. The starting player makes a body movement such as wiggling her nose, clapping her hands, pinching her ears, shaking her head, shrugging her shoulders, or waving her hand— it's her choice. The next player in the circle copies the starting player's movement and adds a new movement. The third player must copy the first two movements in the order they were made and then add a third movement. Play continues in this manner around the circle.

If a player can't remember a movement or copies a movement incorrectly, she is out of the game and must leave the circle. The last remaining player wins.

CREATIVE OPTIONS

• The kids can say words instead of making body movements. Or they can make animal sounds, silly sounds, or even sing a line of a song.

• With kids who are older, play Copy Cat using the alphabet as a guide. For instance, the first player might say, "Apple," the second player, "Bus," and so on through the alphabet with the kids repeating the previous words and adding one of their own. You can coach the kids along by saying "A," "B," or whatever letter they're working on, if they seem to hesitate a little.

• If you'd prefer to play a game that doesn't eliminate players, have the kids sit in a circle and take turns adding a line to a story started by the leader. Ghost stories can be told at a Halloween party and, for a birthday party, a

Materials Needed:
• Enough space for the players to sit in a circle

silly autobiography can be made up about the guest of honor.

PRIZES AND FAVORS

• Provide favors that have a cat theme—cat stickers, stuffed toy cats, or cat posters.

• Give the winner a prize that relates to body awareness, such as the Invisible Man kit, an anatomy poster (available at educational supply stores), or a kids' exercise video.

• If animal or silly sounds are used in the game, choose prizes and favors with an animal theme or make them completely silly—an assortment of joy buzzers, funny spectacles, fake lips and noses, rubber thumbs, and other gag gifts.

TROUBLE-SHOOTING TIPS

• Instead of having players leave the circle if they make a mistake, just say, "Oops, you goofed," and either move on or have the player who missed start a new sequence. There won't be a winner, but the game will still be lots of fun!

• If some players have trouble with memory skills, give them hints or let the other kids give assistance during the game.

• Don't pressure the players to imitate the movements exactly. Some kids are less coordinated than others—accept the best they can do.

SIMON SAYS

Simon Says is traditionally popular with preschoolers, but even preteen players can get fooled by tricky Simon! This game is great indoors and outdoors and keeps kids entertained for long periods of time.

For Ages: 2–5

Optional Ages: 6–12

Players Needed: 3 or more

Object: To follow the correct commands and stay in the game as long as possible

HOW TO PLAY

One player is chosen to be Simon. Simon's job is to call out, "Simon says (describe an action)," while demonstrating the action that the group should mimic.

Everyone in the group must do what Simon says *only* if he begins his command with the phrase "Simon says." If Simon describes and demonstrates an action but doesn't say "Simon says," the group should ignore the command. For instance, if Simon says, "Put your hands on your head," any player who puts his hands on his head is out and must leave the group. (It sounds easy, but many will be fooled!) Another way Simon can trick the other players is by simply doing a movement without saying anything at all. Any kids who copy the movement are out. The faster Simon's commands, the more confused the other players get! The last player remaining wins the game and becomes Simon in the next round.

CREATIVE OPTIONS

• You can play Simon if the group is made up of really young kids. Sometimes playing the role of Simon is difficult, and the kids might find it more fun to be in the main group. Be sure to include some silly commands like "Simon says burp" or "Simon says do a silly dance." This is especially fun and silly when the kids come to the party in costume!

• Have the kids use their own names when calling commands to personalize the game a little. Or use a funny name like "Terminator says . . ." to give them the freedom to giggle and act silly.

Materials Needed:
• Enough space for the players to spread out

• Instead of doing body movements, the kids can use a piece of paper and a pencil to draw the commands. Simon can say, "Simon says draw a circle," "Simon says cross the circle out," "Simon says draw a square," and so on.

• For a larger group, divide the kids into pairs for a team play. The leader gives directions that each team member should do to the other team member—"Simon says mess up your teammate's hair" or "Simon says give your teammate a hug."

PRIZES AND FAVORS

• If you're only playing one round, give the kids who are out a consolation prize while the game goes on—candy, stickers, or small toys work well.

• Give the last remaining player something special—perhaps a T-shirt, videotape, or a gift that goes along with the party theme.

TROUBLE-SHOOTING TIPS

• If you're playing Simon, don't go too fast for the younger kids because it takes them a little longer to process the commands.

• Have some coloring books and crayons set aside to entertain players who are out—this will help them feel better about leaving the game and will keep them busy.

• If a child insists he followed a command, but you saw him make a mistake, give him the benefit of the doubt—after all, it's just a game.

19

OCTOPUS

Octopus is a variation of Tag that's really fast-paced and full of action. You need a lot of outdoor space to play this game. It's a great way for the kids to burn off some extra energy!

For Ages: 2–5

Optional Ages: 6–9

Players Needed: At least 8

Object: To get across the Ocean without being tagged by the Octopus

HOW TO PLAY

Before the game, draw two parallel chalk lines or lay two ropes a good distance apart on the play area. Make sure there is plenty of space for the kids to run around between the chalk lines or ropes (twenty feet is a good minimum distance).

Pick one player to be the Octopus and have her stand in the area between the lines (the Ocean). The other players are the Little Fishes, and they stand behind one of the lines. Their objective is to cross the Ocean and reach the other line without getting tagged by the Octopus.

To start the game, the Octopus yells, "Cross!" and all of the Little Fishes run across the Ocean to safety. Any Little Fish who is caught stays with the Octopus until the next round and becomes a Tentacle. The next round begins when the Octopus yells, "Cross!" and all the Little Fishes run across the Ocean, trying to avoid the Octopus and her Tentacles. Any Little Fish who is caught joins the Octopus and Tentacles. Play continues until the Little Fishes are rounded up.

CREATIVE OPTIONS

- Instead of yelling, "Cross!" the Octopus can call out an item of clothing, and any Little Fish wearing that clothing must cross the Ocean. Or the Octopus can shout out types of pets, and anyone with such a pet must run across—any category will do for this game, so get creative!

- Once they're caught, have the Tentacles stand still in various spots around the Ocean, and allow them to use only their arms and hands to tag the Little Fishes.

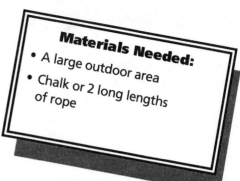

Materials Needed:
- A large outdoor area
- Chalk or 2 long lengths of rope

- For a longer game, let the Tentacles become Little Fishes once they've tagged someone. Play until everyone is too tired to run anymore!

PRIZES AND FAVORS

- Send everyone home with stickers or magnets that have fish on them.

- Give the Little Fishes (and the Octopus) Gummi worms to enjoy after the game.

- Offer the kids "Shark Bites" candies.

TROUBLE-SHOOTING TIPS

- Don't make the play area *too* large or those little legs will get tuckered out too soon. You can easily redraw the chalk lines or move the ropes to suit the activity level of the group.

- Stand behind the goal line so that the kids will be sure to know where to go—you don't want

them running in the wrong direction or into a neighbor's yard!

- If a child gets confused about the clothing item or category called out by the Octopus, help her by whispering or gesturing that she is to run.

- If you're worried about the kids' safety, play on a soft lawn that doesn't have any debris on it, rather than on cement.

GIGGLE AND HOWL

Here's a silly game that puts everyone in a good mood! It doesn't require any preparation and can be played indoors or outdoors.

For Ages: 2–5

Optional Ages: 6–9

Players Needed: 3 or more

Object: To giggle and laugh when the handkerchief is in the air and to keep a straight face when it hits the ground

HOW TO PLAY

The kids stand "frozen" in a circle and can't move until freed by the "magic handkerchief." When you toss the handkerchief up in the air, they must giggle and laugh out loud until the handkerchief hits the ground—then they have to stop *instantly* and become frozen again. If any player breaks into a smile, giggle, or howl after the handkerchief hits the ground, he must leave the circle. Continue until there is only one player left. That player wins the game.

CREATIVE OPTIONS

• Instead of using a plain handkerchief, you can use a small scrap of colorful fabric, a piece of tissue paper, a feather, or a small army figure attached to a toy parachute. You can also blow a soap bubble into the air—when it pops, everyone freezes.

• Use music in place of a handkerchief. Just switch on the music to make the kids come alive and stop the music to make them freeze.

• If you don't want to have a winner for this game, allow the kids who goof to remain in the game, and just keep playing until the kids stop giggling altogether.

PRIZES AND FAVORS

• Offer the kids a home version of Giggle and Howl by giving each of them a colorful bandanna to play with at home.

• Keep the silly mood of the party going by giving everyone a cassette tape of silly songs or a joke book.

• If you use the soap bubble option, give all of the kids a bottle of bubble solution and bubble wands to take home.

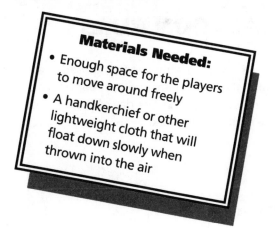

Materials Needed:
- Enough space for the players to move around freely
- A handkerchief or other lightweight cloth that will float down slowly when thrown into the air

TROUBLE-SHOOTING TIPS

- The kids might be unhappy if they have to leave the circle during the game, with so much giggling going on. If this happens, let those kids make faces and act silly outside the circle to make the other kids laugh (without tickling or other physical contact).

- Playing the game outdoors is preferable because the kids will have more room to spread out and run around. If you are playing indoors, clear away the furniture and make sure there's plenty of space for the kids to be able to express themselves.

- If the handkerchief falls too quickly to the ground, hold it from the top of a tall ladder (or piece of furniture if you're indoors) or toss it up in the air wrapped around a small object (toss it away from the kids so the object

doesn't hit anyone). The object will carry the cloth higher up but will detach itself on the way down so the handkerchief floats freely.

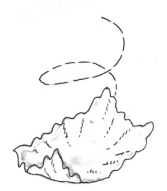

BALLOON BURST

Here's a science experiment disguised as a game that always ends with a "bang." You'll need sunny weather the day of the party or the game won't work.

For Ages: 2–5

Optional Ages: 6–9

Players Needed: 4 or more

Object: To be the first to pop a balloon, using only a magnifying glass

HOW TO PLAY

Before the game, inflate a balloon for each player and tack all of the balloons to a fence that will get direct sunlight during the party hours. Tack the balloons low to the ground, about a foot apart, so the kids can reach them easily. Or use a clothesline, and rig the line low to the ground in a sunny spot and tie the balloons to the line with string.

All of the players sit or kneel in front of a balloon, and on the count of three must hold their magnifying glasses about three inches from the balloon. The sun should shine through the magnifying glasses onto the balloons. After a while, a small bright dot will appear on the surface of each balloon. When this happens, each player must hold her arm and magnifying glass steady until the sun causes her balloon to

pop. The first player to pop a balloon wins. (Don't stop the game once there's a winner— all of the other kids will want to pop their balloons, too.)

CREATIVE OPTIONS

• Let the kids pretend they're scientists during the game—provide accessories such as glasses (without lenses), pens, notebooks, and lab coats (men's white shirts) for everyone.

• For an indoor balloon burst, set the inflated balloons all over the party room floor and let the kids pop as many as they can by stepping or sitting on them.

• If the sun refuses to shine the day of the party, you can still have a balloon burst. Instead of having the kids heat the balloons until they pop, fill them with water and let the kids toss the water balloons back and

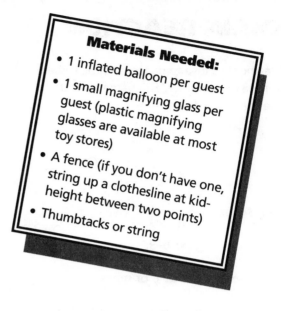

Materials Needed:
- 1 inflated balloon per guest
- 1 small magnifying glass per guest (plastic magnifying glasses are available at most toy stores)
- A fence (if you don't have one, string up a clothesline at kid-height between two points)
- Thumbtacks or string

forth until one eventually bursts, splashing everyone. (To make a water balloon, stretch the opening of a deflated balloon and attach it to a faucet. Holding the bottom of the balloon, turn on the faucet and slowly fill the balloon with water. Turn off the water, take the balloon off the faucet, and tie it closed.) For a really wet time, you can host a water balloon fight. (Just make sure that the guests don't mind a little water and that they bring an extra set of dry clothes.)

PRIZES AND FAVORS

- Give each guest a special Mylar balloon to take home.

- Let the kids keep the magnifying glasses to try the trick again at home.

- Give the game winner a science-related prize, such as a book about the weather or planets.

TROUBLE-SHOOTING TIPS

- Have lots of extra inflated balloons on hand in case any pop accidentally.

- If any kids are afraid of the loud popping noises, let them use tissues as earplugs.

- Sometimes it takes quite a few minutes for the sun to pop the balloons. If this happens, distract the kids with music or a story while they wait.

- Make sure to pick up all of the balloon pieces after any of these games—they can be dangerous around small children and animals.

- Thumbtacks can be dangerous so kids should use them under supervision.

CHAIN REACTION

Preschoolers love to dance, and they love to imitate one another. This game gives them the chance to do both!

For Ages: 2–5

Optional Ages: 6–9

Players Needed: 6 or more

Object: To guess which player is leading the dance

HOW TO PLAY

All of the players should be scattered around the party room in view of each other. Choose one player to be It and have him leave the room while you explain the game to the other players. Then choose one player to be the Dance Teacher.

Start the music so the Dance Teacher can begin a dance move that the other players must imitate. The rest of the players should immediately begin imitating his movements. The player who is It returns to the party room and tries to guess who is leading the dance. The Dance Teacher must keep changing his dance steps throughout the song, little by little, so it isn't obvious who's leading. And the other players should subtly imitate the Dance Teacher without giving away who it is. When the player

who is It guesses who the Dance Teacher is, choose another player to be It and continue playing until everyone has had a chance to lead and to guess.

CREATIVE OPTIONS

• If you're looking for a less-active option, have the kids pretend to be statues, with the leader making a slight movement from time to time and the other players imitating the new pose.

• Seat the kids in a circle and choose one to be the leader and one to be It. The leader should move around a lot (from the waist up). He can clap his hands, pat his head, snap his fingers, or do any movement he wants. The other players must carefully watch the leader and copy everything he does until the player who is It guesses who the leader is.

Materials Needed:
- Enough space for the players to move around freely
- A cassette player and musical tape

PRIZES AND FAVORS

- Give each player a cassette single of a popular song.

- Provide favors that are dance- or music-related—posters featuring famous singers and dancers, music videos, or stickers that have a music theme.

- If you do the statue option, give the players a poseable figure or toy. It's also fun to make a batch of play clay or plaster of paris—the kids can make their own statues!

TROUBLE-SHOOTING TIPS

- Show the kids how to be subtle when imitating the leader. Tell them to *glance* at him once in a while and not to stare, or they will give the secret away too easily.

- Ask for volunteers instead of making each child be the Dance Teacher—some kids might feel shy about leading the group.

- The leaders should change their movements often and not keep one movement going for too long or everyone will get bored. But leaders should not confuse the group by changing their movements too often or too fast.

- If the game seems too easy for your particular group, have the players stand in a circle so it will be more difficult for the player who is It to guess who the Dance Teacher is.

SENSE-SATIONAL

Here's a fun noncompetitive game that preschoolers *love*. It's full of suspense and gives the kids a chance to get "grossed-out."

For Ages: 2–5

Optional Ages: 6–9

Players Needed: 4 or more

Object: To identify each item accurately by touch or smell

HOW TO PLAY

Prepare all of the "touch" and "sniff" items before the party by collecting them in bags and jars. Place the tactile items in zip-lock baggies first (don't seal the baggies) and then in lunch bags, and put the aromatic items in empty containers—cover the sides of the containers with aluminum foil if the labels don't fully hide the contents.

At game time, the players sit in a circle so the items can be passed around easily. Choose one player to start the game and pass the first "touch" item to her. She must reach into both bags and touch the item without looking at it or saying what it is. (The other kids will love watching her expression of surprise or disgust!) She passes the bag to the next player who must touch the mystery item without telling what it is. Once the bag has gone around the circle, the

kids take turns saying what they think is inside. After everyone has taken a guess, pull out the item so the players can see if they guessed correctly, and begin the next round with the new item.

Play the "sniff" version next. This game is played with similar rules—the players must smell each item with their eyes closed and try to identify it.

CREATIVE OPTIONS

• A fun variation is a tasting game where the kids taste a variety of mystery foods and try to identify them. To play, give each child a paper plate and place spoonfuls of mystery food on each one (choose food items that preschoolers will generally like but aren't always easy to identify, such as pizza sauce, frosting, cream cheese, or jelly). The kids have

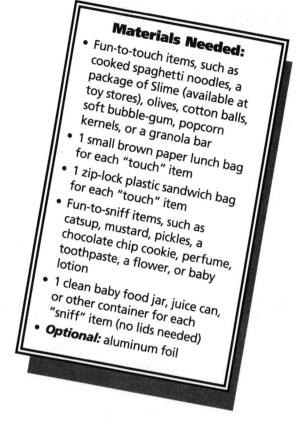

Materials Needed:
- Fun-to-touch items, such as cooked spaghetti noodles, a package of Slime (available at toy stores), olives, cotton balls, soft bubble-gum, popcorn kernels, or a granola bar
- 1 small brown paper lunch bag for each "touch" item
- 1 zip-lock plastic sandwich bag for each "touch" item
- Fun-to-sniff items, such as catsup, mustard, pickles, a chocolate chip cookie, perfume, toothpaste, a flower, or baby lotion
- 1 clean baby food jar, juice can, or other container for each "sniff" item (no lids needed)
- *Optional:* aluminum foil

to taste each item (without smelling it or saying what it is) and then guess what it is once everyone has had a turn to taste.

- Gross the kids out with a game called Body Parts (this is a great game for older kids). Put a bunch of food items in zip-lock plastic sandwich bags and lunch bags, as in the game Sense-Sational, but this time tell the kids you're passing around body parts. (Use skinned grapes for "eyeballs," popcorn kernels for "teeth," cooked noodles for "guts," a small raw carrot for a "finger," and a skinned peach half for a "tongue.") Pass the items around and have the kids reach in and feel the body part. Once everyone has had a chance to touch the items, let them guess what the item *really* is.

PRIZES AND FAVORS

- Send everyone home with some scratch 'n' sniff stickers to wake up their senses.

- If you use Slime as one of your "touch" items, give all of the players a package to take home.

- Offer the kids fun-to-touch items like Koosh balls or Silly Putty.

TROUBLE-SHOOTING TIP

- If a player seems hesitant about touching or smelling anything, let her watch the other players first. She may want to join in later when she sees it's fun to play.

SURPRISE PACKAGE

This game takes some preparation, but it's fun and well worth the effort. It has humor, suspense, and a grand finale!

For Ages: 2–5

Optional Ages: 6–9

Players Needed: 6 or more

Object: To open the surprise package when the music stops and win a special prize

HOW TO PLAY

Before the game, place a grand prize in your smallest box and wrap it in gold gift wrap. Label it "Big Prize Winner!" so the kids will know it's the last box and the best gift. Set the gold box inside a larger box; include a booby prize, candy treat, or small toy, and wrap the package. Repeat until all of the boxes contain one gift, are wrapped, and are stored inside each other. When you're finished you should have one large wrapped box with all of the other boxes and prizes inside it.

The players sit in a circle, and when you start the music, the kids pass the box around the circle as quickly as possible. When you stop the music, the lucky player holding the box is allowed to open it. (Don't tell the kids there are other boxes inside the gift—they'll get the idea

soon enough, which is part of the fun.) Once a player opens a gift he must leave the circle. Play continues with the kids passing the box when the music is started and opening it when the music stops—you may want to warn the kids ahead of time that some of the gifts are a little strange! Soon there will be only two players left. The player who opens the second-to-last box gets to keep its contents and hands the gold grand prize box to the winner.

CREATIVE OPTIONS

- Instead of having a mixture of prizes hidden in the boxes, collect similar, theme-related items such as various candy bars, stickers, or comic books.

- Instead of playing with music, have the kids pick a number from one to twenty. The player

Materials Needed:

- 1 box per player—the boxes should be different-sized and must fit inside each other
- A cassette player and musical tape
- One prize for each player, including inexpensive toys, candy, booby prizes, and a grand prize
- Gold gift wrap, wrapping paper, and ribbon (the Sunday comics can also serve as wrap)
- Scissors
- Tape

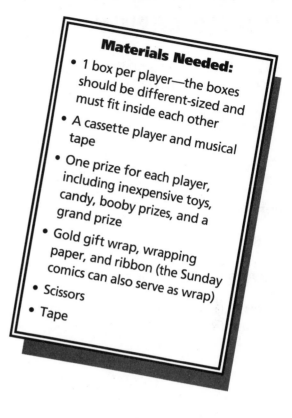

who calls out the selected number opens the box. Continue playing this way until all of the boxes are opened.

- For an added surprise, have the kids close their eyes while passing the package around and then open them when the music stops, to see who got the gift.

PRIZES AND FAVORS

- For the nicer prizes, select candy or other treats, small toys, or board games.

- For the booby prizes, try giant underpants, a pacifier, dog biscuits, or any other silly gift you can think of.

- Choose a popular musical tape, book, or videotape for the big prize winner.

TROUBLE-SHOOTING TIPS

- If the big box is too heavy for the kids to pass around at the beginning of the game, they can push the box around the circle. To avoid this problem, buy lightweight prizes.

- When choosing the prizes, make sure to select generic items that all of the guests will enjoy, especially if there are both girls and boys invited to the party.

HANDY CANDY

No preschooler can resist this game—especially because the game pieces are pieces of candy!

For Ages: 2–5

Optional Ages: 6–9

Players Needed: 4 or more

Object: To guess the number of candies in a handful

HOW TO PLAY

The players gather in a circle around the bowl of jelly beans, and the first player reaches in and grabs a handful. Just when she thinks she gets to keep a whole handful of jelly beans, tell her the rules: she must first guess how many jelly beans she has and can only keep the number she guesses. If she has grabbed ten jelly beans, but guesses that she has five, she must return the extra five to the bowl. If she guesses *over* the amount in her hand, she must return them all and wait for the rest of the players to have a turn before she gets another try. Play continues until everyone has a handful.

CREATIVE OPTIONS

• Give everyone a special candy bag at the beginning of the party and attach it to their clothes with safety pins or to their belt loops

with string. The kids can save their candy to take home.

• Place four different-sized bowls, one inside the other, on the floor with the kids gathered around them. Label the smallest center bowl "4," the next largest bowl "3," the next largest bowl "2," and the largest "1." Distribute ten jelly beans to each player. While kneeling, each player tosses the jelly beans into the bowls, trying to reach the bowl labeled "4" in order to get four points. At the end of each turn, see where the jelly beans landed and assign points based on the bowl numbers. For instance, two jelly beans in bowl "3" would be six points. When the points are all added up at the end of the toss, give the player that amount of jelly beans as a prize.

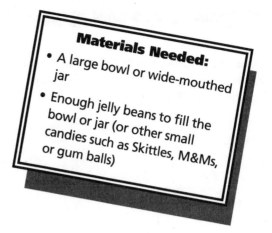

Materials Needed:
• A large bowl or wide-mouthed jar
• Enough jelly beans to fill the bowl or jar (or other small candies such as Skittles, M&Ms, or gum balls)

• Hang Lifesavers from the ceiling with string and tape, and let the kids try to eat them.

PRIZES AND FAVORS

• Send everyone home with a variety of candy.

• Give each child a bag of gourmet jelly beans.

• Other fun favors are stickers, memo pads, or toys with a candy theme.

TROUBLE-SHOOTING TIPS

• Be sure the kids wash their hands before playing since they'll be handling all the candy. Or, to avoid sticky hands, play the game using small wrapped candies instead of jelly beans.

• One way to avoid having the kids eat too much candy during the party is to tell them they can eat their candy *only* when they hear the "candy bell" ring (you can use a bell or whistle for this purpose). If they are caught eating their candy at any other time, they must put one piece of their candy in the "candy pot" (a bowl or dish). Split the candy in the candy pot between all of the guests at the end of the party.

LOOSE AT THE ZOO

This version of tag is fun for kids because they really have to stay alert! It's a good outdoor game for an active bunch.

For Ages: 2–5

Optional Ages: 6–9

Players Needed: 6 or more

Object: To reach the other side of the line before getting caught by the Zookeeper

HOW TO PLAY

Before the party, cut out pictures of different zoo animals from magazines or coloring books (or draw them yourself) and glue them onto index cards. Make one animal card for each player. Then draw two parallel chalk lines or lay two ropes a good distance apart on the play area (twenty feet is a good minimum distance).

Select one player to be the Zookeeper—the rest of the kids are the Zoo Animals. The Zookeeper stands between the lines while the other players stand behind one of the lines. The Zoo Animals are each given an index card that tells them which animal they should pretend to be for the game. They should keep their animal identities from the Zookeeper.

The Zookeeper patrols the Zoo (the play area), walking back and forth between the rope or

chalk lines and making sure there are no loose Zoo Animals. At the same time, the Zookeeper must shout out the names of different zoo animals—any he can think of. Players whose cards match the animals called out must run to the opposite side of the play area before the Zookeeper tags them. Any child who is caught must freeze instantly, and all the other kids must run loose *around* him for a more challenging race. Any kids who make it to the other side go back to the starting line for another round. The game is over when all the animals have been frozen—the very last Zoo Animal to get caught is the winner.

CREATIVE OPTIONS

• For added fun, make a bunch of extra index cards with different animals on them so that the kids who make it across the line without

34

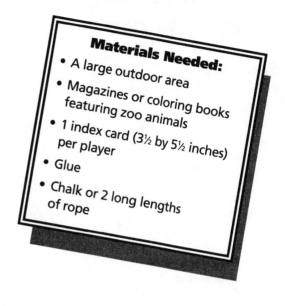

Materials Needed:
- A large outdoor area
- Magazines or coloring books featuring zoo animals
- 1 index card (3½ by 5½ inches) per player
- Glue
- Chalk or 2 long lengths of rope

getting caught can become a new animal right away and continue playing.

- Instead of having the kids who are tagged freeze, let the Zookeeper "lock up" the tagged kids behind the finish line with a special key—these kids can even act like caged animals so they won't get bored!

- Give the Zookeeper a prop to use (a special shirt, hat, or name tag) while he's in the middle of the field.

PRIZES AND FAVORS

- Give the kids small plastic or stuffed animals, animal coloring books, or animal masks to take home.

- Let the kids have any props used in the game.

- Give the grand prize winner a special theme-related prize, such as a big stuffed animal.

TROUBLE-SHOOTING TIPS

- Before the Zookeeper begins calling out animal names, give the kids a few moments to memorize which animal they are so they don't have to keep looking at the pictures.

- If the Zookeeper is too quick and always catches the other players, have him turn his back to the group, call out an animal, and then quickly turn around to catch runners.

- If you're worried about the kids' safety, play on a soft lawn that doesn't have any debris on it, rather than on cement.

DINOSAUR DIG

All kids love dinosaurs, so they'll be thrilled with this activity, which lets them dig for "dinosaur bones." For extra fun, plan a whole dinosaur party with dinosaur decorations and "prehistoric" food!

For Ages: 2–5

Optional Ages: 6–9

Players Needed: 2 or more

Object: To dig for "dinosaurs" and find the special prize

HOW TO PLAY

Before the party, bury some "bones" (pipe cleaners or popsicle sticks) in a sandbox or a sand-filled roasting pan. Also bury a special treat—toward the bottom of the sand so it takes longer for the kids to find it—and if you're using more than one roasting pan, hide a treat in each one so all of the kids have a chance at finding the prize.

Give the kids spoons, strainers, or shovels and tell them to pretend they're archaeologists digging for dinosaurs. Let them know there's one special item hidden in the sand, and that whomever finds it is the grand prize winner.

Once the kids have uncovered all of the bones, they can put together their dinosaurs. If they're using pipe cleaners, they can twist and shape the pipe cleaners into spines and ribs and bend

the pipe cleaners around one another for legs and feet. With popsicle sticks, all they need is some glue and imagination. Award ribbons (made from posterboard and colored with felt-tip pens) to each dinosaur when the activity is finished—under categories like "most creative," "scariest," or "best built." Display the dinosaurs and ribbons on a table in the party room for everyone to enjoy.

CREATIVE OPTIONS

- Hide plastic dinosaurs in the sand rather than "bones." Let the kids keep any they find.

- Hide a plastic Easter egg filled with jelly beans (call it a big dinosaur egg filled with lots of mini dinosaur eggs)—the player who finds it is the grand prize winner.

- Decorate the party room to look like a prehistoric land by hanging up pictures of

Materials Needed:
- Pipe cleaners or popsicle sticks (about 10 per child)
- A backyard sandbox or a large foil roasting pan filled with sand (1 pan for every 3 kids)
- Spoons, small strainers, or small plastic shovels
- A special treat that is well-wrapped (like a miniature candy bar, a small sticker pack, or a pack of bubblegum)
- Glue (if you're using popsicle sticks)
- Posterboard
- Felt-tip pens

dinosaurs cut out from construction paper and lining the table with plastic dinosaurs, along with the kids' dinosaur-bone creations. Place a dark paper tablecloth over a large table (or two small ones pushed together) so that it falls completely to the floor. Let the kids (or cave people) enjoy their party refreshments as they hide in this makeshift cave!

PRIZES AND FAVORS

- Let the kids keep their homemade dinosaurs or any other dinosaurs found in the sand.

- Pin the ribbon awards on the guests for them to wear home.

- Give everyone plastic or rubber dinosaurs.

- Send the grand prize winner home with a book about dinosaurs, a pack of dinosaur stickers, or another item featuring dinosaurs.

TROUBLE-SHOOTING TIPS

- Tell the players that archaeologists dig very carefully and that they should, too. That way the kids won't toss sand everywhere and make a mess in their excitement to find "bones" and prizes.

- If the kids will be constructing dinosaurs from pipe cleaners or popsicle sticks, have a few dinosaur books handy so the kids can copy them, rather than trying to create them from memory.

- If some of the kids don't find enough "bones" to create a dinosaur, have a few extras on hand to give them.

FUNNY PAPER RACE

The comics section of the Sunday newspaper is great for party activities—and it's inexpensive to use. This funny paper race gives the kids a chance to act silly!

For Ages: 2–5

Optional Ages: 6–9

Players Needed: 6 or more

Object: To cross the finish line before the rest of the players

HOW TO PLAY

Cut out a bunch of popular characters from the Sunday comics—two of the same character for each player. Cover the cut-outs with clear Contact paper or glue them to 3½-by-5½-inch index cards so they'll be sturdy enough to last the whole game. Then place one of each character into two separate boxes.

At game time, the kids line up side by side, facing the finish line (twenty feet is a good minimum distance—or choose a distance you feel is appropriate for the group). Make a finish line out of the Sunday comics for added fun!

Without looking, each player picks a character from the first box. Then the first player in the line chooses a character from the second box and shows it to the group. The player whose character matches the one picked gets to move toward the finish line by taking a step appropriate to the character. If the player's character is Garfield, he could take a step forward on all fours, meowing. If his character is Fred Flintstone, he could take a step forward and yell, "Yabba-Dabba-Do!" The player who chose the character then returns it to the box, and the next player in the line chooses one. (Bring the characters to the kids as they move closer to the finish line, so they won't lose their place.) The game continues until one player has crossed the finish line—that player is the winner.

CREATIVE OPTIONS

• Make necklaces out of the cartoon cards by punching two holes at the top of each one. Reinforce the area around the holes with tape, and string yarn through the holes (or let the kids do this at the party). The kids can

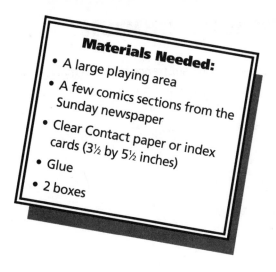

Materials Needed:
- A large playing area
- A few comics sections from the Sunday newspaper
- Clear Contact paper or index cards (3½ by 5½ inches)
- Glue
- 2 boxes

keep one cartoon identity throughout the race or trade necklaces.

- Instead of using the Sunday comics, buy coloring books that feature many different cartoon characters and let the kids color the pictures before the race.

PRIZES AND FAVORS

- Give each player a comic strip character covered in clear Contact paper to take home and make up several more so the kids will have lots to play with. They're fun to use in the bathtub!

- Give the kids items featuring favorite comic strip characters like Garfield, Snoopy, or Opus—Mylar balloons, T-shirts, stuffed toys, and play figures are popular.

- Pass out comic books to everyone and give the grand prize winner a gift certificate to a store that specializes in selling them.

TROUBLE-SHOOTING TIP

- Some kids may be less coordinated than others, so don't emphasize competition in this race—the kids will enjoy the challenge of the race just as much without the competition.

39

MAGIC "MOOSH"

This fascinating substance is fun to make and will intrigue the kids for a good part of the party. And if you're careful, it won't even make a mess!

For Ages: 2–5

Optional Ages: 6–9

Players Needed: Any group size

Object: To make a magic concoction

WHAT TO DO

Set up a big table (outdoors, if possible, to prevent a mess), and cover it with newspaper. The kids can stand up while making the "moosh" if there aren't enough chairs. Hand out sandwich bags and let the kids pick out a favorite shade of food coloring. When everyone has their materials, begin demonstrating the following steps, pausing often and checking that the kids are following directions properly: (1) Pour 1 cup cornstarch into the sandwich bag, and slowly add approximately ¼ cup water mixed with a few drops of food coloring, (2) Carefully press the excess air out of the sandwich bag and seal it shut, and (3) Knead the sandwich bag until the mixture is well-blended and smooth, but don't puncture the bag!

Watch their delight as the kids mix up the "magic" concoction, which slowly changes from dry to wet, from hard to soft, and from white to a color. Tell the kids to first squeeze the mixture firmly and quickly in the bag and then feel the mixture "melt" in their hands.

CREATIVE OPTIONS

• The kids can add two different shades of food coloring to the "moosh" to make a new color.

• Let everyone put glitter in the "moosh," at the same time the food coloring is added, for a little sparkle.

• Another fun and magical recipe is a catsup and mustard creation that the kids can work with to make designs. Just put a blob of catsup and a blob of mustard in a zip-lock plastic sandwich bag for each child, seal it,

Materials Needed:
- A large table
- 1 cup cornstarch per child
- About ¼ cup water per child
- Food coloring (many colors)
- 1 zip-lock plastic sandwich bag per child

and let the kids create colorful designs by pressing or "drawing" on the baggies with their fingers. The two colors will stay separated for a while. Once they've completely mixed, pour the contents into a bowl and use this special sauce to top hot dogs, burgers, or french fries.

PRIZES AND FAVORS

- Make fun "moosh" recipe cards for everyone so they can try the activity again at home.

- Give everyone some store-bought or home-made play dough to take with them.

TROUBLE-SHOOTING TIPS

- To be on the safe side, seal the sandwich bags with electrical tape to make sure they won't open during handling.

- If you have a large group, premeasure the materials so that all the kids have to do is pour and mix.

- Although the "moosh" mixture is nontoxic, it's not a good idea for the kids to put it in their mouth. Warn them ahead of time to touch but not taste.

- Provide the kids with old T-shirts to put over their clothing so the food coloring won't stain their good clothes.

41

CATERPILLAR CRAWL

In this activity the kids not only get to make their own caterpillar, but also make it crawl. It gives them a chance to create and control their own tiny world for a while—they'll love the experience.

For Ages: 2–5

Optional Ages: 6–9

Players Needed: Any group size

Object: To create a caterpillar and "magically" make it crawl

WHAT TO DO

Set up the materials at a table—this will make it easier for the kids to work on their projects. The kids can start by making either the caterpillar or the caterpillar's tail. To make the caterpillar, they need to tightly coil a pipe cleaner around a pencil. The coil should be about two inches long. While the pipe cleaners are still on the pencils, have the kids glue two wiggly eyes onto one end of the pipe cleaners. Set the caterpillars aside so the glue can dry.

Using felt-tip pens and crayons, the kids can create a winding caterpillar trail or maze on cardboard or paper plates. Encourage the kids to get creative and make a whole caterpillar environment with grass, flowers, rocks, and anything else they can think of.

When the trails are done, have the kids remove their caterpillars from the pencils and stick a piece of magnetic tape (cut to about one inch) on the underside of the caterpillars. Then show the kids how to bring the caterpillars to life! By holding a magnet underneath the cardboard surface and putting the caterpillar over the magnet, it will magically scurry along the cardboard trail as the magnet is moved.

CREATIVE OPTIONS

- For more "advanced" caterpillars, have the kids glue together three pom-poms, apply wiggly eyes, and use pipe cleaners for the antennae.

- Rather than using pieces of cardboard or paper plates, the kids can use shoeboxes or even larger-sized boxes. Just prepare the boxes ahead of time by cutting out the sides, leaving a two-inch border by each box corner.

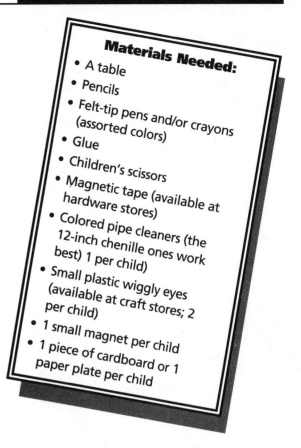

Materials Needed:

- A table
- Pencils
- Felt-tip pens and/or crayons (assorted colors)
- Glue
- Children's scissors
- Magnetic tape (available at hardware stores)
- Colored pipe cleaners (the 12-inch chenille ones work best) 1 per child
- Small plastic wiggly eyes (available at craft stores; 2 per child)
- 1 small magnet per child
- 1 piece of cardboard or 1 paper plate per child

Turn the boxes over and use the flat surface. The kids can reach up under the box, which resembles a table, to control the magnet and caterpillar. The benefit of using a large box is that four kids can use the box at once.

- Host an insect party—with the guests dressed as favorite bugs! Serve "insect" refreshments, such as sundaes with "chocolate-covered ants" (chocolate sprinkles) and "bugs on a log" (celery sticks spread with peanut butter, with rows of raisins on top).

PRIZES AND FAVORS

- Let the kids keep their caterpillars, trails, and magnets to take home and play with—the caterpillars make good refrigerator magnets.

- Give everyone a small metal toy to use with their trails.

- Offer coloring books with an insect theme,

books about insects, or a homemade "bug catcher" for studying bugs (a fancy jar with holes poked in the lid and a ribbon tied around the mouth).

TROUBLE-SHOOTING TIPS

- Test the magnets before the day of the party to be sure they're strong enough to work through a piece of cardboard.

- If you're using a cardboard box or a piece of cardboard box, make sure it's not too thick and has no seams. A thin, smooth surface works best.

- For safety, help the kids when they're using scissors.

- The magnets and small plastic wiggly eyes are dangerous if swallowed—supervise the kids carefully.

DAFFY DRESS-UP

It doesn't have to be Halloween for kids to dress up and pretend they're someone (or *something*) else. All they need are funny clothes and accessories, and a little imagination.

For Ages: 2–5

Optional Ages: 6–9

Players Needed: Any group size

Object: To encourage creativity and make-believe play

WHAT TO DO

To set up, just toss a bunch of clothes in a big, lidded box and cover it with wrapping paper so it looks like a giant gift. Then let the kids open it at once and pull out the clothing. Bring out some accessories and tell the kids they can dress up in the fancy clothing and pose in front of the mirror to their heart's content. You'll probably have to help them with the accessories, especially putting on make-up. Encourage creativity, and let the kids be as silly as they want.

Once the guests have on outfits they're happy with, let them have a parade. They'll love marching through the neighborhood modeling their new clothes—just go a short distance, like around the block. Let them keep their dress-up outfits on throughout the rest of the party, if

they wish. It will be fun for them to act like grown-ups during refreshments and other party activities.

CREATIVE OPTIONS

- Have the kids dress each other, with half of the kids posing as "department store mannequins" and the rest of them playing "window dressers." Then let them switch roles so all of the kids are dressed up.

- Help the kids do a little skit after they're dressed up. They'll love pretending!

- Videotape the parade or take Polaroid snapshots of the kids in costume so they can see how funny they look.

Materials Needed:
- All sorts of fun adult clothing: flannel shirts, harem pants, sports or occupation uniforms, high-heeled shoes, oversized boots, floppy hats, and sailor caps (available at thrift shops, costume shops, and from your own closet)
- All sorts of accessories: wigs, scarves, fake jewelry, ribbons, ties and bow ties, and make-up (available at thrift shops)
- A full-length mirror
- A large cardboard box
- Wrapping paper (the Sunday comics can also serve as wrap)
- Tape

PRIZES AND FAVORS

- Before the dress-up activity, make some little award certificates or ribbons—one for each guest. These can be as simple or creative as you want. Label these awards with categories such as "silliest outfit," "most creative costume," or "most imaginative." Be sure they're all positive so that all the kids feel special.

- Give everyone their Polaroid snapshot.

- Give out favors that go along with the dress-up theme, such as T-shirts that feature a special party message or paper dolls.

TROUBLE-SHOOTING TIPS

- Be sure to have a wide variety of interesting and unique clothes for the dress-up activity. Don't collect clothing appropriate to only one gender—it limits creativity.

- On the invitations, tell everyone to wear snug-fitting clothes to the party, such as tights, bathing suits, or exercise wear, so they can easily put the dress-up clothes over their own.

MAKING WAVES

You've heard of a ship in a bottle—here's an "ocean in a bottle." This simple, unique activity is fun to do, and the end result is a long-lasting toy that kids will really enjoy.

For Ages: 2–5

Optional Ages: 6–9

Players Needed: Any group size

Object: To create a homemade toy that really lasts

WHAT TO DO

Before the party, wash and dry one bottle and cap for each child. If there are labels on the bottles, soak the labels in warm water for a half hour and try to peel as much of them off as you can.

Gather the kids at a table with the materials spread out before them. Using a funnel, pour six ounces of cooking oil into each child's bottle, followed by six ounces of vinegar. Let the kids observe the fluids interacting—the oil goes to the top and the vinegar to the bottom. Then pour several drops of blue food coloring into the bottles, and again let them watch the changes and separations.

Close the caps tightly and tell the kids to shake their bottles to make "waves." For added fun, give everyone tiny plastic toys to put inside the mixture so they can float in a homemade ocean. Plastic confetti and glitter will add sparkle, too. Once all of the materials are added, seal the caps shut with rubber cement or glue to prevent leakage.

CREATIVE OPTIONS

• The kids can make a tornado in a bottle instead of waves. The easiest way is by first purchasing a "Tornado Tube" (under three dollars at most educational supply stores) for each guest. Then clean out two large clear plastic soda bottles for each child and have the kids fill one of their bottles up with water and a pinch of glitter. Attach the "Tornado Tubes" to the bottles according to the package directions, and tell the kids to swirl the water-filled bottle and watch the tornado appear.

Materials Needed:
- A table
- 12-ounce plastic bottles with screw-on caps (1 per child)
- 6 ounces of cooking oil per child
- 6 ounces of vinegar per child
- Blue food coloring
- Glitter, plastic confetti (available at party supply stores), or tiny plastic toys
- A funnel
- Rubber cement or strong glue

• Send invitations with a beach theme. Seal zip-lock plastic sandwich bags (filled with either water or sand) with some glue, and attach a piece of paper with the party details on it. You'll need to hand-deliver these!

• Decorate the party room with homemade starfish and seaweed cut out from construction paper and serve the food with plastic shovels. You can also serve a cake decorated like the beach.

PRIZES AND FAVORS

• Let the kids keep their new "wave makers."

• Give everyone water toys, such as pails and shovels, squirt guns, bathtub body paints, or small plastic boats.

• Offer books about tornadoes or send everyone home with their "Tornado Tubes."

TROUBLE-SHOOTING TIPS

• Tell the kids that, like the ocean, the liquids in the bottle aren't liquids they should drink. (The ingredients are nontoxic, but warn the kids anyway.)

• Glitter and plastic toys are dangerous if swallowed—supervise the kids carefully.

47

MYSTERY PUZZLE PIECES

Here's a quiet activity with a surprise twist. The identity of the person in the "mystery puzzle" always comes as a delightful surprise to the party guests—it's them!

For Ages: 2–5

Optional Ages: 6–9

Players Needed: Any group size

Object: To solve the identity in the mystery puzzle

WHAT TO DO

Before the party, collect photographs of all the guests scheduled to attend. You'll need to do this secretly, so call the guests' parents to arrange it. Suggest that they supply more than one photo so you can pick the one that will reproduce the best.

Take the photos to a copy store to have them reproduced in black and white and enlarged to a small poster size (about twelve-by-eighteen inches). Cut posterboard to the size of the photocopies and then spray the pieces of posterboard with spray adhesive. Next, lay the enlarged pictures of each guest on the posterboard, pressing down firmly. Allow the posters to dry for a few minutes, cover them with clear Contact paper if desired, and draw large-sized puzzle shapes on each one using a black felt-tip pen. Then cut out the puzzle pieces, keeping them together, and slip each puzzle into a large envelope. You can write each child's name on the inside flap of the envelope so you'll know which puzzle belongs to whom.

When you're ready for a quiet-time activity during the party, pass out the envelopes and have the kids put the puzzles together. Tell them the finished result will be a special surprise. Wait until you see their expressions when they realize the face on the puzzle is their own!

CREATIVE OPTIONS

- If the puzzles aren't covered with clear Contact paper, the kids can color them with crayons.

- Serve a cake decorated with the race of the honored guest (call a bakery for details).

Materials Needed:
- A photograph of each child (school photos work well, or try to get one that features a full-body shot)
- 1 large sheet of posterboard per guest
- Spray adhesive
- A black felt-tip pen
- 1 large envelope per child (bright and colorful, if possible)
- Scissors
- *Optional:* clear Contact paper

• Another fun activity to do with the kids' school photos is to create a "Miniature Me" for each guest. Using a set of paper dolls, trace the paper doll on a large piece of posterboard several times. Make photocopies of each guest's headshot and glue the photocopy of each photo onto each paper doll's head. For a fun, quiet activity, present the kids with their very own miniature likenesses and let them color them in. They can also add glitter or other decorative items—let their creativity run wild!

PRIZES AND FAVORS

• Give the kids special gift certificates at a shop that creates magazine covers, T-shirts, or mugs featuring the customer's likeness.

• Send the kids home with their personalized puzzles and paper dolls.

• Many bookstores have storybooks, activity books, and coloring books with an "all about me" theme—these would make fun favors.

• Take Polaroid snapshots of the kids during the party and present them in small, inexpensive frames.

TROUBLE-SHOOTING TIP

• Be sure to make the puzzle pieces large enough for preschoolers to use. If they have too many pieces to work with, the activity won't be as much fun.

DOWN ON THE FARM

A nearby farm makes a great outing for a preschool party. Let those citified party-goers have a look at things they may not see too often—cows giving milk, pigs getting fed, or a farmer driving a tractor.

For Ages: 2–5

Optional Ages: 6–9

Preparation: Look in the Yellow Pages for farms that are open to the public and arrange a visit. Or ask your child's preschool teacher to recommend one.

WHAT TO DO

To get the kids in the mood for a trip to the farm, read them a story about farm animals or farming before you go, and sing a few verses of "Old MacDonald" during the drive.

Once you arrive, the owners of the farm or a farmhand will probably guide the group around (request this specifically when you call, if you wish), so just follow along and enjoy the experience. Ask ahead of time if it's possible to arrange some special activities, such as allowing the kids to milk a cow, brush the horses, pick some berries or corn, feed the hens, gather eggs, ride on a tractor, or take a hayride. Some farm owners provide tours of the house and barn, or they let the kids get involved in some of the easier farm tasks— others might just want the kids to watch. No matter what the day brings, the kids will have a wonderful time being outdoors and seeing the animals in their picture books "come alive." Don't forget to bring a camera!

CREATIVE OPTIONS

• Find out if the farm you're visiting offers pony rides or maintains a fish hatchery, for added fun.

• While at the farm, give the kids some tasks to do as they tour the facilities. For example, give each child a different quest, such as finding out what kind of food the horses eat, what sound a goat makes, or how many cows there are. Have them share their discoveries on the car ride home.

• Send invitations cut out in the shape of farm animals, with a little plastic farm animal attached. Ask the guests to wear "farm" clothing (flannel shirts, jeans, and wide-

For Added Fun:
- Storybooks about farm animals or farming
- A cassette tape featuring "Old MacDonald"

brimmed hats) so they blend right in with the scenery.

- Back at the ranch, serve food like pork and beans, hot dogs, and apple cider, with a cake featuring plastic farm animals grazing on a meadow of green-tinted frosting.

PRIZES AND FAVORS

- Give the kids Polaroid snapshots of themselves with the animals to take home.

- Offer everyone plastic farm animals or a cassette featuring "Old MacDonald."

- If you can find some coloring books featuring farm animals or Golden Books that tell farm stories, give them to the kids as a memorable follow-up to their rural adventure.

TROUBLE-SHOOTING TIPS

- Get adult volunteers to accompany you on the outing to make sure the kids don't get hurt or wander off with a herd of cows. Never leave a child unattended on a farm!

- Before you leave for the farm, go over a few simple rules: no yelling because it might startle the animals, no running because it will stir up the dust, and no touching the animals unless permission has been given.

- Tell the kids to wear old clothes so they won't have to worry about mud or dirt.

- Use the buddy system on this outing—have the kids hold hands with a partner so they'll stay together.

ZOOMING TO THE ZOO

Kids and animals go together like cake and ice cream, so a day at the zoo will be a big hit with preschoolers!

For Ages: 2–5

Optional Ages: 6–9

Preparation: Call the zoo ahead of time to find out the hours of operation and to see if there are any special exhibits or shows that preschoolers might enjoy.

WHAT TO DO

If you have a plan of action ready before the kids arrive, the event should go smoothly. Preschoolers have a short attention span (and short legs!), so make sure they won't be walking around the zoo for more than about two hours. Choose the most exciting exhibits, and save time for the petting zoo, if there is one. If you plan to have cake and ice cream at home after the outing, give everyone little goody bags to take along to the zoo, so the kids won't want to stop each time they see a snack bar. Fill the bags with "animal" foods like peanuts, bananas, berries, and nuts. (Just make sure they don't try to give the goodies to the animals!)

Collect the kids together for a ride in the "zoo-mobile" to make the drive more fun, especially if the zoo is far from your home. Put a few bars made from black construction paper on the car windows and a sign in the rear window that reads: "Zoo-mobile—Do Not Feed the Animals." The kids will love singing animal-related songs like "I'm Being Swallowed by a Boa Constrictor" or "Five Little Monkeys Jumping on the Bed" and making animal noises.

At the zoo, keep the group together with simple planned activities. The kids can make the sound of each animal they see or walk and behave like animals as they go by the exhibits. Point out the various kinds of foods the animals eat, their habitats, and their different movements. After the zoo tour, have a picnic on the grass or open the goody bags and then head home for cake. Some zoos sponsor parties for kids, so you can have cake, ice cream, and the works right there—just call for a reservation.

For Added Fun:
- 1 small brown paper lunch bag per child
- A mixture of peanuts, bananas, berries, or nuts

CREATIVE OPTIONS

- Let the kids make animal masks to wear on the excursion or dress up in homemade animal costumes.

- Arrange for a special guided tour around the zoo, if possible.

- Books about zoo animals are fun to share with preschoolers, before and after the outing.

- Set up the party room to look like a zoo by drawing cages and animals on large sheets of paper and hanging them on the walls.

PRIZES AND FAVORS

- Send the kids home with animal stickers, animal coloring books, animal crackers, and small plastic animals.

- Let everyone pick out one special (but inexpensive) item from the zoo's gift shop.

- Bring along a Polaroid camera and take pictures of each guest in front of a favorite animal or exhibit. Give out the pictures at the end of the party as a special memento.

TROUBLE-SHOOTING TIPS

- Mention on the invitation that the kids should dress in casual clothes (appropriate for the weather conditions on the day of the party) and comfortable shoes.

- Make name tags for everyone (decorate them with animal stickers, if you wish) or assign partners so that nobody will get lost.

- For a large group of kids, ask other parents to attend the event and help keep everyone together and under control. If you can't round up any volunteers, arrange for a trusted babysitter to come along.

PUMPKIN PATCH PARTY

If you're planning a fall party, include a trip to a pumpkin patch and let the kids pick out their very own pumpkins to creatively carve and decorate.

For Ages: 2–5

Optional Ages: 6–9

Preparation: If you don't know the location of a pumpkin patch in your area, look in the Yellow Pages under "Orchards" to find one. Find out the hours of operation, the costs, and get directions to the field.

WHAT TO DO

On the invitation, request that the kids wear orange and green clothing (this will make it easier to keep track of everyone) or that they come in some sort of a pumpkin costume. Then, on the way to the pumpkin patch, keep the kids entertained with songs or stories.

When you arrive at the patch, let the kids explore the area, examine all the pumpkins, and pick out their favorite. A fun additional activity is a Pumpkin Hunt. Secretly put stickers on some pumpkins while the kids are wandering in the pumpkin patch. Once all the kids have chosen a pumpkin, send them back in the field to look for the special pumpkins with stickers on them. Tell them that whomever finds a sticker wins a prize (let the winner keep the extra pumpkin and give them each a sticker pack, too).

Plan extra time for pumpkin-carving/decorating activities after the trip, if you wish. Just put newspaper on a table for pumpkin-carving and show the kids what to do. Don't give them knives or other sharp objects—there are safe pumpkin-carving utensils at drugstores and grocery stores. It's also a good idea to draw faces on the pumpkins before doing any carving. Half the fun of this activity is opening the pumpkin shell and pulling out all the yucky stuff, so be sure to allow the kids to do this. Or for a less messy activity, give the kids colorful permanent felt-tip pens and let them draw faces on their pumpkins.

CREATIVE OPTIONS

• Here's a different pumpkin-decorating activity: cut up a bunch of vegetables and store them until you're ready to get started. Then let the kids use the vegetables to make

For Added Fun:
- Stickers
- A table
- Newspaper
- *Safe* pumpkin-carving tools or permanent felt-tip pens

faces on their pumpkins—use radish slices for eyes, a carrot stick for a nose, some bell pepper slices for a mouth, and celery tops for hair. Attach the vegetables with straight pins or thumbtacks (*supervise this activity!*).

- Rinse the pumpkin seeds once you scoop them out of the pumpkins. Bake the seeds on a cookie sheet in the oven at 350° for about five minutes (until they're crisp and lightly browned). Then let the kids gobble them up for a tasty snack. The seeds can be toasted plain, or shake on a little salt or other seasoning before baking to give them extra flavor.

- Invite the kids to the party by hand-delivering miniature pumpkins with the party details written on them with felt-tip pen, or mail the guests pumpkin-shaped invitations cut out from orange construction paper.

PRIZES AND FAVORS

- The personalized pumpkins make great mementos of the party.

- Send the kids home with small bags of candy corn and packaged pumpkin seeds or let them take the freshly-baked seeds.

TROUBLE-SHOOTING TIPS

- Adult supervision is necessary not only for the pumpkin-carving but also for decorating pumpkins with vegetables.

- If you plan to let the kids carve their pumpkins, it might be easier to have an adult volunteer help you with this project. That way, the kids won't get bored or frustrated waiting for help.

SCIENTIFIC EXPEDITION

Here's an exciting expedition into the fun side of science—an adventure that will fascinate the kids through hands-on experience.

For Ages: 2–5

Optional Ages: 6–9

Preparation: Most cities have a kids-style science museum that offers lots of science activities for kids to explore. Look in the Yellow Pages under "Museums" to find one near you. Call ahead of time to find out the hours of operation, costs, directions, and whether they have guided tours, group rates, or special classes.

WHAT TO DO

Give each guest a fun science toy to play with on the ride to the museum—a magnet, magnifying glass, telescope, kaleidoscope, prism, or other science gizmo—this will keep them busy and get them in the mood for their educational adventure.

Once you arrive at the museum, let the kids walk around and enjoy the science exhibits and displays. Let them look at everything, independently or in pairs, depending on their preference. After allowing enough time to see the exhibits, break for an activity called "What If." For this game you'll need to have prepared ahead of time a list of "What if . . ." questions. Write down questions that will get preschoolers thinking about fantastic possibilities— "What if your cat could talk?" "What if trees grew money?" "What if it rained popcorn?"

or "What if you could fly like a bird?" Give everyone a chance to answer and share their ideas. When it's time to leave, stop by the museum gift shop to get the kids a special (but inexpensive) science toy to play with on the ride home.

CREATIVE OPTIONS

• Allow extra time for doing some fun "science" experiments at home. Here's a good one: Give each child a glass of water— the amount of water in the glasses should vary. Show the kids how to make music by holding the glass steady with one hand, dipping a fingertip of the other hand in the water, and lightly rubbing the fingertip in a circular motion around the rim of the glass. The trick is to use slight pressure—it will produce a ringing sound. The sounds will be higher- or lower-pitched depending on the amount of water in each glass.

For Added Fun:
- Small science toys
- Paper
- A pencil or pen

- Let the junior scientists make some tasty peanut butter play dough! Mix together two cups smooth peanut butter, two cups powdered dry milk, and one cup honey. (You can double the recipe for a larger group.) The result will be a pliable and edible substance that the kids will love.

- If you plan to do a few science-related activities after the trip to the museum, have the guests come dressed in white lab coats (men's white shirts).

PRIZES AND FAVORS

- Give the kids a gift certificate to a store specializing in science and nature gifts.

- Offer do-it-yourself science activity and experiment books (available at bookstores). Two fun ones are James Lewis's *Measure Pour & Mix, Kitchen Science Tricks* and *Learn While You Scrub, Science in the Tub,* published by Meadowbrook Press.

- If you try the peanut butter play dough option, let everyone take a sample home in a baggie—if they haven't already eaten it, that is! Or write up the recipe for each child to try again at home.

TROUBLE-SHOOTING TIPS

- Keep a close eye on each child while visiting the museum. Ask the guests to wear red or yellow T-shirts to the party (the bright colors will be easy to spot) and provide giant name tags for all the guests with the address and phone number of the party host, in case anyone gets lost.

- Find adult volunteers to help on the trip because the kids will want to run off in different directions. If you can't round up any volunteers, arrange for a trusted baby-sitter to come along.

UNDER THE SEA

Some kids may hate eating fish, but all kids love looking at fish—so why not plan an "under the sea adventure?"

For Ages: 2–5

Optional Ages: 6–9

Preparation: If you live in a big city, you probably have an aquarium nearby. Call ahead of time to learn the hours of operation, costs, directions, and whether they have guided tours, group rates, or special classes. If there isn't an aquarium in your area, you can still have an "under the sea" party. Look in the Yellow Pages under "Fish Hatcheries" and plan a different outing that's just as fun.

WHAT TO DO

When the guests arrive, have them make "fish" to take along to the aquarium. Give everyone a mitten to decorate, with the fish's face at the fingertip end of the mitten and the fins at the knitted end. Using felt-tip pens, puffy paints, felt scraps (preferably pre-cut into small shapes), accessories, and any other art materials, the kids can create colorful, imaginative sea creatures. Once the decorations have dried, the kids can slip the fish mittens onto one hand and wiggle them to make the fish "swim." Some kids might prefer to make sharks—the thumb area of the mitten can serve as the fin.

When you arrive at the aquarium, let the kids explore the various exhibits, under supervision. If the aquarium also features a tide-pool area, feed-the-fish tank, or deep-sea diver show, be sure to visit these attractions. After viewing all the aquarium has to offer, head home, keeping the kids entertained with songs from the movie *The Little Mermaid*.

CREATIVE OPTIONS

- If there's time for more fun after the outing, play a new type of "Go-Fish" with the kids, tossing a fishing pole line (a stick with string attached, and a magnet on the string) behind a couch or chair and "catching" metal toys—Matchbox cars, metallic figurines, or refrigerator magnets.

- Decorate the party room walls with lots of fish cut out from colored construction paper, blue waves made from crepe paper, and creepy rubber sharks and octopuses (avail-

For Added Fun:
- 1 white (or any light colored) cotton mitten per child (available at hardware stores)
- Permanent felt-tip pens
- Puffy paints (available at art supply stores)
- Accessories such as ribbons, sequins, glitter, buttons, or felt scraps
- Glue

able at toy stores) hung with thumbtacks. For a hazy "underwater" effect, replace your regular light bulbs with blue or green ones and cover the lamp shades with inexpensive shades poked with tiny holes so the light peeks out.

PRIZES AND FAVORS

- Give the kids their homemade fish mittens and toys from the "Go-Fish" game.

- Give everyone items related to *The Little Mermaid* movie such as small figurines, books, and soundtrack cassette tapes.

- Let the kids pick out an inexpensive item from the aquarium gift shop.

TROUBLE-SHOOTING TIPS

- Use the buddy system on the outing—have the kids hold hands with a partner so they'll stay together.

- Depending on the size of the group, you might want to ask other adults to accompany you. If you can't round up any volunteers, arrange for a trusted babysitter to come along.

- Be sure the kids know they shouldn't tap on the glass at any of the aquarium exhibits (or disturb the fish at the hatchery). Reward those who behave well with stickers.

CLOWNING AROUND

All kids love to clown around! Turn your party into a really special event by inviting a professional clown to entertain!

For Ages: 2–5

Optional Ages: 6–9

Preparation: Find a clown by looking in the Yellow Pages under "Entertainers—Entertainment" or in kids' magazines. For a less-expensive alternative, arrange for a friend or family member to do the job. (Clown suits and make-up are available at costume shops.)

WHAT TO DO

You can find a clown through a special company or agency, or you can hire one that works independently. Interview several by phone ahead of time to determine which performance or act is right for your party and guests. Some clowns use props, and some pass out balloons or party favors.

Your clown party can be fun and simple—just let the clown do the entertaining and then have cake and ice cream afterwards. Videotape the performance if possible, and let the kids watch it once the clown leaves, for an added treat.

If you have extra time for preparation, provide the kids with clown accessories and let them dress up for the special guest. They'll have loads of fun putting on colorful oversized

clothes, funny shoes, wild wigs, and floppy hats. Put make-up on each child (you may want to invite another adult to help you with this), or if the guests are a bit older, let them make up themselves or each other. Once the clown leaves, have a parade, take lots of photos, and enjoy the kids' show.

CREATIVE OPTIONS

• Turn the party room into a big top circus! Create booths out of cardboard boxes, decorate the party area with streamers, hang pictures of clowns and circus animals on the walls, and play circus music in the background (the music of John Philip Sousa will work well). Have a special face-painting booth for turning the guests into clowns.

• Invite guests to the clown party with balloon invitations that they have to inflate to read

For Added Fun:
- Wigs
- Colorful shirts
- Baggy pants
- Oversized shoes
- Floppy hats
- Rouge
- Eyeliner
- Eye shadow
- Lipstick
- "Clown white" make-up (These materials are available at costume shops, thrift shops, or drugstores.)
- A camera or videocamera

(write the party details on inflated balloons, deflate, and mail).

- Serve hot dogs or corn dogs for the main refreshment, and popcorn and peanuts for a snack. Serve a "circus" cake shaped like a carousel and covered with brown sugar "sawdust" and plastic horses.

PRIZES AND FAVORS

- Give everyone a Polaroid snapshot of themselves dressed as a clown before they leave.

- Pass out helium-filled or Mylar balloons.

- Give each guest a book or coloring book about the circus.

- Provide bags of peanuts or popcorn.

TROUBLE-SHOOTING TIPS

- Some kids are afraid of clowns—all that make-up and wild clothing can be scary—so explain to them what the clown will look like and that a clown is really a person in disguise. Some clown entertainers might also be willing to clean off their make-up and change clothes in front of the kids when they're done performing—kids find the transition amazing.

- If the kids will be dressing up like clowns, have them draw their clown faces on paper first so they'll have a good idea how they'll look. Encourage a lot of creativity—traditionally, no two clown faces are supposed to look alike!

FIRE FIGHTER! FIRE FIGHTER!

Kids love the hero image of a fire fighter, and many local fire stations are happy to send someone over to talk with the kids, show them the equipment, and teach fire safety.

For Ages: 2–5

Optional Ages: 6–9

Preparation: Call a local fire station to see if a fire fighter can come to the party in uniform with some equipment.

WHAT TO DO

When you call the fire station, find out what items the fire fighter can bring for the presentation (such as fire-fighting equipment, handouts, or posters). Be sure to determine the amount of time the fire fighter will be able to spend at the party—if it's a short time, plan other activities.

As the guests arrive, give them fire-fighter hats to wear. Encourage them to ask the fire fighter questions if they want. When the special presentation is over, gather the kids for a "fire check" activity. Have the group walk around the house and yard searching for possible (but imitation) fire hazards that you have set up ahead of time—piles of newspaper, a gas can, matches—and award a sticker for each potential hazard found. After the fire

check, have the kids create a fire safety poster using posterboard and felt-tip pens, with a thank-you message for their favorite fire fighter. Then load the kids into the car, and drive to the fire station to drop it off.

CREATIVE OPTIONS

- Ask the fire fighter if it would be possible to arrive in a fire truck (one of the small ones) that the kids can explore, under supervision, during the party.

- Have the kids act out a skit involving a fire scene with some of them pretending to be fire fighters and some of them needing to be rescued.

- Send out invitations in the shape of a fire hat or fire truck.

For Added Fun:
- Fire-fighter hats for each guest (available at toy stores)
- Posterboard
- Felt-tip pens
- Stickers

- Decorate the party room with ladders, hoses, fire-fighter hats, and axes—all made from construction paper.

PRIZES AND FAVORS

- Let the guests wear their fire-fighter hats home and keep any items the fire fighter passed out during the presentation.

- Give everyone a book or coloring book about fire fighting or fire safety.

- Pass out bags of red hot candies.

- Give the kids dalmatian dog stuffed animals.

TROUBLE-SHOOTING TIP

- Remind the kids to be good listeners when the guest arrives, and reward those who listened quietly with a special sticker.

'TOON TOWN

Mickey and Minnie Mouse, Fred Flintstone, the Tasmanian Devil—all are favorites with kids. Your guests will love watching a cartoon character come to life!

For Ages: 2–5

Optional Ages: 6–9

Preparation: You can hire a costumed cartoon character for your event through special companies and agencies listed in the Yellow Pages under "Entertainers—Entertainment." For a less-expensive alternative, arrange for a friend or family member to rent a cartoon character outfit from a costume shop.

WHAT TO DO

If you plan to hire a cartoon entertainer through a special company or agency, find out what kinds of services they will provide. Some entertainers will have a special act, and some offer photo and videotaping services. If you plan to have a friend dress up, you'll need to have games and activities—the "special guest" can join in the party rather than put on a show.

Encourage the kids to ask the visitor questions (yes or no questions are best), shake hands, or give hugs. The character can pass out favors, too. For the main event, take Polaroid snapshots of each guest sitting on the lap of the special entertainer.

Later, have the kids make their own creative cartoon panels using white posterboard cut into six-inch squares. They can color a back-ground scene with the felt-tip pens or crayons and fill in the scene with the cartoon characters from comic and coloring books (cut these out before the party so the kids won't be using scissors). They can either glue the characters onto the scene for a display or do creative play by moving the characters around. When the cartoon panels are complete, the kids can arrange them in an interesting sequence and make up a connecting story.

CREATIVE OPTIONS

• Rent a favorite cartoon video if you have a VCR. Disney movies are popular, but short cartoon videos are also available.

• Purchase a coloring book featuring some favorite cartoon characters, cut a few different characters out, and place them in a large envelope. At game time, pull out a

little bit of the character at a time, and have the kids try to be the first to guess who it is.

• Purchase a cartoon coloring book and cut one scene up into large puzzle-shaped pieces (one piece for each child). Give each guest a piece of the puzzle to color with felt-tip pens. To play, place the pieces in a large envelope, have one child reach in and pull out a puzzle piece and guess what character it might be, and then place the puzzle piece on the table. Repeat this with all of the guests, having them try to connect the pieces as the game progresses. Continue until the cartoon character is revealed and the puzzle is put together.

• Invite the guests with homemade cartoon character invitations. The party details can be placed in a speech bubble.

PRIZES AND FAVORS

• Let everyone take home the Polaroid snapshot of themselves with the special guest.

• Give the kids comic books, cartoon coloring books, small plastic cartoon figurines, or stickers featuring cartoon characters.

• Video rental stores often have cartoon posters or inexpensive cartoon movies that would make fun favors.

TROUBLE-SHOOTING TIPS

• If any guests are frightened by the larger-than-life cartoon character, take them aside and privately explain that it's just a person dressed up in a costume.

• To keep the kids from wrestling over the cut-out cartoon characters for their cartoon panels, make sure you have extra cut-outs of the most popular characters on hand.

TELL ME A STORY

Stories hold a magical quality for everyone—especially children. A storyteller can bring magic to a party—and it's usually an inexpensive form of entertainment.

For Ages: 2–5

Optional Ages: 6–9

Preparation: Contact a children's bookstore, library, or preschool for storyteller referrals.

WHAT TO DO

True storytellers are a real treasure. They make up stories or tell them from memory, with a lot of movement and expression. Depending on the situation, you may be able to request a specific story, arrange for a telling of several preschool-level stories, or have the storyteller dress up as a character. If you are unable to find a storyteller for the party but would still like to have one, arrange for a friend or family member to play the role. Have a few practice runs before the party for a smoother, more animated reading. To get the kids in the mood for a story, request on the invitation that they dress as their favorite story character and bring a favorite book to the party.

Plan some special activities to do after the storyteller is finished. The kids can take turns telling the other guests which character they are dressed up as or acting out the story their character is from (videotape this, if possible). Then let the kids create their own storybook (using blank books you've prepared ahead of time by covering pages made from plain white paper with covers made from tagboard). Poke some holes about two inches apart where the bookbinding would normally be and tie all of the pages together with yarn. The kids can draw scenes on the pages with pencils, crayons, and felt-tip pens. If there's time, read to them from storybooks they brought, or show them the videotape you made.

CREATIVE OPTIONS

• Serve a storybook cake shaped like an open book, with frosting words and illustrations.

For Added Fun:
- Tagboard
- Plain white paper
- A hole-punch
- Felt-tip pens
- Pencils
- Crayons
- Yarn

- Show a selection from Shelley Duvall's *Faery Tale Theatre* after the storyteller has gone.

- Invite the kids to the party with invitations made to look like miniature storybooks.

- Decorate the party room with books and posters from a library or children's bookstore.

PRIZES AND FAVORS

- Send everyone home with a special book as well as their own homemade book.

- Offer posters that promote reading or feature storybook characters.

- Give each child a bookmark.

TROUBLE-SHOOTING TIPS

- To promote good listening, remind the kids not to talk or disturb the storyteller during the presentation.

- If any of the kids are inattentive during the story, let them quietly draw pictures that go along with the story.

- Some younger children will need individual attention while making their storybooks. Older guests can pair up with younger ones to offer help and encouragement, or parents can help their youngsters.

MAKING MUSIC

"Come to a party!" can be music to a child's ears—especially if the party promises a musical entertainer. Invite a professional musician or singer to entertain the kids for a really memorable event.

For Ages: 2–5

Optional Ages: 6–9

Preparation: You can hire a musical entertainer through special companies and agencies listed in the Yellow Pages under "Entertainers—Entertainment." For a less-expensive alternative, invite a friend or family member with special talent to entertain. Or call a preschool or a music store for musician or singer referrals.

WHAT TO DO

If you plan to find a musician or singer in the Yellow Pages, be sure to ask if the entertainer performs music that preschoolers will enjoy. If someone you know will be doing the entertaining, have a few practice runs to make sure the performance will go smoothly. See if your musical guest can bring along some preschool songs and fingerplays to teach the kids. The entertainer could also bring a few musical instruments to share and cassette tapes or videos that feature performers for the very young (or provide these materials).

Plan lots of activities before and after the performance. The guests can perform songs or fingerplays or play musical instruments and form a little band (videotape this, if possible). If you don't have any real musical instruments,

let the kids create some. They can make drums from oatmeal canisters, maracas from spice bottles and dried rice or beans, and kazoos from empty toilet paper rolls with one end covered with waxed paper and secured with a rubber band. After the musical guest leaves, show the kids the videotape you made. Or let the kids can listen to music and dance.

CREATIVE OPTIONS

• Show a video featuring lots of music, such as *Annie* or *Beauty and the Beast*.

• Have the kids take turns being a "one-man band," playing as many instruments as possible—all at once!

• Invite the guests with a musical invitation—a card in the shape of a musical note, a harmonica, or a kazoo with the party details tied on.

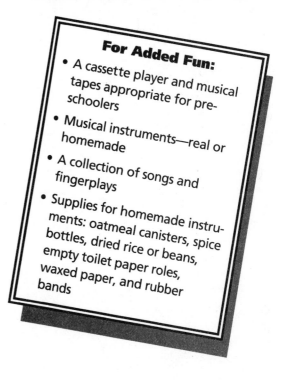

For Added Fun:

- A cassette player and musical tapes appropriate for pre-schoolers

- Musical instruments—real or homemade

- A collection of songs and fingerplays

- Supplies for homemade instruments: oatmeal canisters, spice bottles, dried rice or beans, empty toilet paper roles, waxed paper, and rubber bands

- Request that the guests bring along their favorite cassette tape or a musical instrument to play at the party if they have one, so they can share the music they love.

- Play a round of Musical Chairs if there's any extra time (see p. 12 for directions).

PRIZES AND FAVORS

- Let the kids take their homemade instruments with them when they leave.

- Give everyone an inexpensive musical instrument to take home such as a kazoo, harmonica, or set of musical spoons.

- Offer cassette tapes of popular children's songs or videos featuring a famous singer.

TROUBLE-SHOOTING TIPS

- Be sure you have an instrument for every guest so no one is left out. If that's not possible, supervise to make sure the kids take turns.

- Don't worry about musical ability—this party is bound to sound a little off-key sometimes. Instead, focus on enhancing cooperation between the members of the "band," watching the kids learn new skills, and letting them have fun with music.

School Age 6-9

GUMBY LOTTO

Gumby Lotto is a homemade version of the popular party game Twister. Kids love this game because it gives them a chance to get all tangled up like a Gumby doll!

For Ages: 6–9

Optional Ages: 2–5, 10–12

Players Needed: 3 or more

Object: To be the last remaining player on the board

HOW TO PLAY

Prepare the Gumby Lotto board by painting a grid on a plastic sheet with twenty-four squares, each twelve-by-twelve-inches wide (six-by-six-inches for younger kids). Then paint a different sticker design, using the sticker packs as a guide, inside each square. Cut tagboard or paper into twenty-four small squares and put a different sticker on each one—these will be the playing cards.

When the guests arrive, place several different stickers from the matching sticker set on their hands, feet, elbows, and knees, making sure each player gets the same number of stickers. At game time, have the first player choose a card. The card must match one of the stickers on her body in order for her to move onto the board—if it doesn't match, the card is passed to the next player or on down the line until

someone has a match. When a match is made, the player must put the body part on the corresponding Gumby Lotto square. For instance, if a player has a matching sticker on her elbow, she must bend over and put her elbow on the grid. Play continues with the players taking turns putting their hands, feet, elbows, and knees on the board as cards are chosen (keep shuffling and reusing the cards). If a player is unable to get a body part in the appropriate square or loses her balance, she is out. The last remaining player on the board wins.

CREATIVE OPTIONS

• If you don't have time to make the game materials, purchase the board game Twister at a toy store instead.

• Videotape the kids getting all tangled up with each other and show the video later. Or take Polaroid snapshots—one for each guest.

Materials Needed:
- A large sheet of clear or white plastic, about 6 feet long (an old shower curtain or plastic bedding will work)
- Acrylic paints
- 2 sets of 24 matching stickers with simple designs
- Tagboard or paper
- Scissors

• After a few rounds of Gumby Lotto, use the plastic grid as an English Hopscotch board. Just use six of the squares, and have the kids hold a marker (a rock, rubber ball, or any small object) between their feet while taking turns jumping through the path of squares.

PRIZES AND FAVORS

• Give everyone a sticker pack to take home.

• If you play Hopscotch, give each of the kids a small toy to use as a marker such as a fancy eraser, key chain, or rubber ball.

• Give the winner of Gumby Lotto the board game "Twister."

TROUBLE-SHOOTING TIPS

• Be flexible with the rules so the kids will have a good time. If a player chooses a card that doesn't match any of her stickers or simply can't reach a square, allow her to choose another card for a second chance.

• Lay the grid on a soft surface so the kids won't get hurt when they topple over during the game.

SUITCASE RELAY

This relay race will have everyone laughing! It's especially fun for going-away parties, but it will be a big hit at *any* party.

For Ages: 6–9

Optional Ages: 2–5, 10–12

Players Needed: 6 or more

Object: To be the first team to reach the finish line after completing the required challenges

HOW TO PLAY

Before the game, pack two suitcases with a collection of crazy, mismatched clothing, making sure that each carryall has an equal amount of clothes. Divide the kids into two teams, with the same amount of players on each side, and set up a starting line and goal line (twenty-five yards between the two lines is a good distance)—masking tape or pieces of rope work well for this.

To start, the kids line up in their teams and the first player in each line runs toward the goal carrying a suitcase. When those two players reach the goal line, they open their suitcases, put on *every* item of clothing, pick up the empty suitcases, run back to the starting line, undress, put all the clothes back in the suitcases, close them, and hand them off to the

next teammates in line. The next players repeat these steps, passing the suitcases on to the next kids in line. All the players have to do is put the clothing items on their bodies—it's okay if they wear flippers on their hands or put a shirt on backwards (it's a race for fun, not to see who can correctly dress themselves). The game continues until one team has finished the race—that team is the winner.

CREATIVE OPTIONS

• A variation is to divide each team in half and have one half stand at the first line and the other half stand at the second line. The race starts with the first players on each team opening the suitcases, putting on the mismatched clothing, closing the suitcases, and running to their teammates at the other line. The same players then take off the clothes, and the first teammates waiting at

Materials Needed:
- 2 small suitcases, tote bags, or brown paper grocery bags
- Crazy, mismatched clothing, including footwear (high heels, galoshes, or even flippers), an oversized item (a big shirt, smock, or coat), and a funny accessory (goggles, mismatched knee-high socks, or a bathing cap)
- Something to mark the starting line and goal line (masking tape or pieces of rope work well)

the other line pack the clothing into the suitcases and sprint back to the first line. The race continues until every player has had a chance to pack and dress, and the quicker team wins.

- For a simpler race, have the first runners pack the suitcases with items you've provided (clothing, accessories, toiletries—anything goes), carry the suitcases to the goal line, run back to the starting line, unpack the suitcases, and hand them off to the next players. The game continues until the faster team finishes.

PRIZES AND FAVORS

- Give everyone a funny accessory to remind them of the race—goggles, flippers, a bathing cap, or a pair of silly socks.

- Offer each child an inexpensive lunch box (a mini suitcase). Put goodies like candy and bubblegum inside, for an added surprise.

- Make travel goody bags for the kids by filling small brown paper lunch bags with gum, mini bags of peanuts, little activity books, or toy vehicles like cars or trains.

TROUBLE-SHOOTING TIPS

- For younger kids, have extra adult helpers on hand in case any of the kids have trouble putting the clothes on.

- Avoid clothing items that might be difficult to put on such as belts, turtleneck shirts, or long underwear.

TWENTY QUESTIONS

Twenty Questions is a classic game that's fun to play in a large or small group. Try some variations to give the game a new twist.

For Ages: 6–9

Optional Ages: 10–12

Players Needed: 3 or more

Object: To guess the person, place, or thing within twenty yes or no questions

HOW TO PLAY

Before the game, write the names of real or fictional people, places, or things on cards cut from tagboard. You can add an element of humor to the game by labeling the cards with people, places, or things that will make kids laugh—the Terminator, the Principal's office, or underwear.

The first player chooses a card (without looking at the other cards) and tells everyone whether her secret word is a person, place, or thing. One by one, the other players ask yes or no questions to figure out the answer. The group can only ask a total of twenty questions. Each player can try to solve the mystery when it's her turn, but an incorrect guess means she's out of the game. (An incorrect guess doesn't count toward the twenty questions.)

Continue to play until twenty questions have been asked. If no one has guessed correctly by then, the card-holding player reads the answer and wins a prize for stumping the group. Anyone who guesses the correct answer within the twenty questions wins.

CREATIVE OPTIONS

• Let each player come up with a person, place, or thing rather than putting the answers on cards.

• Instead of using person, place, and thing categories, play the game using animal, vegetable, or mineral categories. (This version works better with older kids.)

• Play a version of Twenty Questions called Virginia Woolf. The players must select famous people, living or dead, for everyone to guess.

Materials Needed:
- Tagboard
- A pencil or pen
- Scissors

- If the kids really like the game, you can break them up into pairs and let them play Twenty Questions quietly together—perhaps while everyone is waiting for parents to arrive at the end of the party.

PRIZES AND FAVORS

- Send each guest home with a small wrapped box with a secret "thing" inside. Fill the boxes with candy or small toys.

- Give the kids postcards, posters, or buttons featuring famous celebrities. Make a game of it and have them guess what their prizes are, one at a time, before they go home!

- Give each guest twenty stickers, twenty gum balls, or twenty wrapped hard candies.

TROUBLE-SHOOTING TIPS

- To make the game easier, have the player holding the card give a hint after every question. For instance, if someone guesses "Is he famous?" and the answer is yes, a hint such as "But he's only famous if you watch TV" can be given. The game will move faster, and the kids will win sooner. You can even write up some hints ahead of time on the back of the cards.

- If the kids have trouble guessing the correct answers within twenty questions, allow them to just keep guessing until everyone gives up.

BLIND MAN'S BLUFF

How well do the party-goers really know their friends? This fun game will help them find out! Blind Man's Bluff is best-suited for a large group of kids that know each other.

For Ages: 6–9

Optional Ages: 10–12

Players Needed: 8 or more

Object: To guess the identity of another player while blindfolded

HOW TO PLAY

Choose one player to be the Blind Man and blindfold him. (When you blindfold children, make sure the blindfold isn't too tight and that it covers their eyes completely.)

All of the players form a circle around the Blind Man with their hands joined. The players start moving in one direction until the Blind Man claps three times. At that time, the players in the circle must stop, and the Blind Man points to one of them and is given one guess to name that person. If the Blind Man guesses correctly, the two players switch places, and if he guesses incorrectly, the player steps into the middle of the circle with the Blind Man.

The Blind Man stays blindfolded and tries to catch his chosen player, who in turn tries to avoid being caught. Once the Blind Man catches the player in the circle, he must try to identify the player by touching the player's clothing, hair, and other features (the player must stand still while the Blind Man does this). When the player is correctly identified, the Blind Man removes the blindfold and joins the circle, and the identified player becomes the Blind Man. Play continues until everyone has taken a turn being the Blind Man.

CREATIVE OPTIONS

• During the chase part of the game, the child in the circle with the Blind Man can make funny sounds to attract—or distract—the Blind Man.

• A fun variation eliminates the chase part of the game—instead, the players move in a circular motion around the Blind Man, while singing a song of their choice. When the

Materials Needed:
• Enough space for the players to form a wide circle
• A blindfold, bandanna, large scarf, or eye mask with the peepholes covered with black construction paper

song ends, the Blind Man points to one of the players and gives a funny command such as "Howl like a wolf," "Sing like Michael Jackson," or "Talk baby talk." The Blind Man then tries to identify the player, and if he does, the two switch places. Otherwise, the game continues with the players circling and singing again.

• Let the Blind Man touch only the hands, clothing, face, or hair of the player in the circle to make guessing more difficult.

PRIZES AND FAVORS

• Give everyone a bandanna "blindfold" to take home.

• Take Polaroid snapshots of each player as the Blind Man and give the photos as souvenirs at the end of the party.

• Offer all of the kids cassette singles of popular songs.

TROUBLE-SHOOTING TIPS

• Make sure the play area is free of any obstacles (like furniture or lawn debris) so the kids won't trip or hurt themselves.

• If a child is reluctant to wear a blindfold, let him be the last to take a turn so he can see it's not too threatening. If he still refuses, allow him to play with his eyes closed.

• If the game is too difficult with the Blind Man getting only one guess, allow three guesses instead.

UP, JENKINS!

This classic game hasn't gone out of style with today's kids because it has all the suspense, excitement, action, and surprise that kids love.

For Ages: 6–9

Optional Ages: 10–12

Players Needed: 8 or more

Object: To discover which player has the hidden coin

HOW TO PLAY

Divide the players into two teams and have them sit on opposite sides of the table. Pick one child on each team to be the leader and give one team a coin. Have a piece of paper and a pencil handy for keeping score.

To start the game, one team begins passing the coin back and forth among each other, underneath the table. After a short period of time, the leader of the other team shouts, "Up, Jenkins!" The team with the coin must quickly raise their closed fists above their heads. The leader of the other team then shouts, "Down, Jenkins!" and the team with the coin slaps their opened hands on the table, palms down. The team without the coin should listen carefully for the coin hitting the table so they can identify the player who is concealing the coin. (They can discuss their guesses in secret before announcing who they think the culprit is.)

One by one, the leader of the team without the coin says the names of the players on the opposing team, trying to eliminate those players who *don't* have the coin. When a player's name is called, she must lift her palms from the table to show the coin isn't there. If the coin is revealed before the last player's name is called, that team gets to hide it again. However, if the team correctly identifies the culprit, the players on that team take the coin to hide.

Play as many rounds as possible in an allotted amount of time (twenty minutes or so) and give each team a point when they identify the culprit correctly. The team with the most points wins.

Materials Needed:
- A table
- A coin
- A piece of paper and a pencil or pen

CREATIVE OPTIONS

- To make the game more difficult, have the guessing team identify the person who has the coin *and* which hand the coin is in.

- Instead of calling "Up, Jenkins!" the kids can shout "Up, Chuck!" to add a little humor to the game.

- Use a jellybean instead of a coin so that the kids will get a giggle when it gets flattened on the table. (You'll need a plastic tablecloth or a card table that can be wiped off for this option.) Replace the squished jellybean with a fresh one after each round.

PRIZES AND FAVORS

- Give all of the kids gold foil-wrapped chocolate coins to eat at the party or take home.

- If you try the jellybean option, offer small bags of jellybeans or other candy.

- Send everyone home with a couple of real coins and a small piggy bank.

TROUBLE-SHOOTING TIPS

- Tell the kids not to slap the table *too* hard or their hands will be sore!

- If you're using a table with a wood finish, place a padded tablecloth on it to prevent scratches and to cut down on noise.

- Demonstrate how to slap your hand on the table without dropping the coin or letting it slip out.

PENNY PITCH

The sport of pitching pennies goes way back, but it's still lots of fun. And the game pieces (a handful of pennies) are always easy to find.

For Ages: 6–9

Optional Ages: 2–5

Players Needed: 3 or more

Object: To pitch and win the most pennies

HOW TO PLAY

Put ten pennies in a paper cup for each player (write the players' names on the cups to avoid confusion during the game). Then spread ten extra pennies on the ground (or floor, if you're playing indoors) in front of a wall.

At game time, give each player a cup of pennies and tell the first player to gently toss a penny against the wall, aiming it so the penny will ricochet and hit one of the pennies on the ground. If the tossed penny touches one of the pennies on the ground, the player who made the toss retrieves his penny and the one he hit. (If the tossed penny touches more than one penny on the ground, the player may keep all the pennies hit.) However, if the shot is missed, the player loses the tossed penny (it stays on the ground where it lands), and the next player takes a turn. Play continues until all of the pennies are emptied from the cups or all of the pennies are gone from the ground. The player who has the most pennies at the end of the game wins.

CREATIVE OPTIONS

• Draw a grid on a large piece of paper and put it on the ground in front of the wall. Mark some of the squares with stars, some with circles, and some with triangles (or any design will do). Then fill small brown paper lunch bags with candy or small toys and mark each bag with one of the designs in the grid. Any time a player's penny lands in one of the boxes containing a design, let him reach into the bag with the corresponding design for a prize.

Materials Needed:

- A wall
- 10 pennies per child, plus an extra 10 pennies
- 1 paper cup or other container per child
- Enough space for the kids to spread out
- A pencil or pen

- Instead of spreading only pennies on the ground, include a variety of different coins—nickels, dimes, quarters, half-dollars, and even some fake coins or wooden nickels.

- Allow the players to continue tossing pennies if the tossed penny hits another penny, stopping only when their coins miss the mark.

PRIZES AND FAVORS

- Let the kids keep all of the coins won during the game.

- Give everyone a collection of gold foil-wrapped chocolate coins to eat during the party or to take home.

- Give the winner a piggy bank for storing his winnings.

TROUBLE-SHOOTING TIP

- Show the kids how to toss the pennies gently and take aim—the pennies will tend to bounce off the wall and roll away if thrown too hard.

AIRPLANE

Here's a fun game for older kids that's a variation of Pin the Tail on the Donkey. They'll love the suspense!

For Ages: 6–9

Optional Ages: 10–12

Players Needed: 6 or more

Object: To pin your airplane to the map, farthest from the "takeoff" spot

HOW TO PLAY

Before the game, make an airplane for each player by cutting airplane shapes out of tagboard (write the players' names on the airplanes to prevent confusion over who wins). Hang a map on the wall of the party room and mark a "takeoff" spot in the middle of it.

At game time, line up the players at the opposite end of the room from the map and, while they're watching, put several obstacles in the middle of the room (furniture, throw pillows, or wastebaskets will work well—nothing breakable!). Give the players some time to study the placement of the obstacles and the "takeoff" spot.

One by one, hand the players an airplane, blindfold them, and point them toward the map. (When you blindfold children, make sure the blindfold isn't too tight and that it covers their eyes completely.) Each player must cross the floor without touching any obstacles and pin the airplane to the map as far away from the "takeoff" spot as she can. If a player runs into an obstacle before reaching the map, it's considered a plane crash and the player is out. If she reaches the map but pins her airplane to the water, it's considered a crash-landing and she is out. The player who reaches the map safely and pins her airplane farthest from the "takeoff" spot is the winner.

CREATIVE OPTIONS

• Provide crayons, paint, glitter, and other art supplies and let the kids decorate their airplanes before the game. Or let the kids create their own fantasy maps.

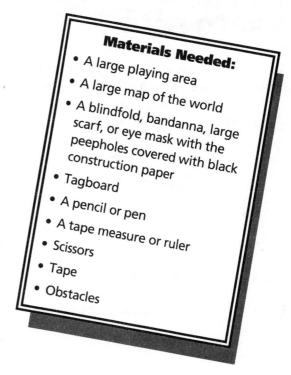

Materials Needed:
- A large playing area
- A large map of the world
- A blindfold, bandanna, large scarf, or eye mask with the peepholes covered with black construction paper
- Tagboard
- A pencil or pen
- A tape measure or ruler
- Scissors
- Tape
- Obstacles

- Spin the kids around before their turn so they get even more mixed up about where to go. (Don't spin them too hard or too long!)

- For an easier game, just have the kids try to reach the map and pin their plane on it rather than trying to avoid the water, too.

PRIZES AND FAVORS

- Let the kids take their airplanes home.

- Give each child a colorful map of the United States.

- Offer everyone toy airplanes or airplane stickers (available at toy and discount stores).

- Give the kids bandanna "blindfolds."

TROUBLE-SHOOTING TIPS

- When setting up the obstacles, make sure you don't use any small items the kids could trip over or low tables they could bang their knees on. Encourage them to walk across the room slowly so they won't get hurt.

- If a child is reluctant to wear a blindfold, let her be the last one to take a turn so she can see it's not too threatening. If she still refuses, allow her to play with her eyes closed.

MARCO POLO

Marco Polo is a classic game for a pool party. If you don't have a swimming pool, play the game in the shallow end of a public pool—with lots of adult supervision.

For Ages: 6–9

Optional Ages: 10–12

Players Needed: 3 or more

Object: To avoid being caught by Marco

HOW TO PLAY

Choose one player to be Marco. He must close his eyes and count to ten, giving the other players a chance to scatter throughout the pool. Then, with his eyes closed, he must find and tag one of the other players.

To find the other players, Marco swims blindly around the pool, calling out "Marco!" to which the other players respond all at once, "Polo!" Marco can call out as often as he likes—even if he is inches from one of the other players—and the other players *must* respond. Once Marco tags another player, that player becomes Marco, and the game begins again. The kids will probably want to play many rounds!

CREATIVE OPTIONS

• Play a "silent" version of the game with Marco calling out "Marco!" and the players responding with movement only. The players can swim, splash, or gently ripple the water—Marco must listen very carefully to find the others.

• Have one player be Jaws! All of the players, including Jaws, must close their eyes. Jaws swims around the pool trying to "attack" the other players. With everyone "blind," the tension and suspense increases.

• If you're playing at a public pool, have the kids stay in the shallow end only. (A larger shallow end can be a fun advantage, too—more space to hide in!)

Materials Needed:
• A swimming pool

PRIZES AND FAVORS

• Give all of the kids a pair of swimming goggles to wear during the party and take home later.

• Send everyone home with favors that remind them of a fun day at the pool—a pair of sunglasses, beach ball, water toy, snorkel, or flotation device.

• If you try the "Jaws" option, offer the kids Shark Bites candy and shark toys.

• Give everyone a beach towel to use at the pool and to take home.

TROUBLE-SHOOTING TIPS

• Adult supervision is vital for all pool activities. If you have a large group, make sure you have more than one lifeguard.

• Call all of the guests' parents ahead of time to find out if their kids can swim. Ask any parents of weak swimmers to provide flotation armbands and make sure the kids wear them.

• Provide sunscreen for all of the kids, and encourage them to apply it frequently.

TUG OF WAR

A good old-fashioned Tug of War is a great way to help kids work off their excess party energy. Half the fun is losing as one team tumbles to the ground in a laughing heap!

For Ages: 6–9

Optional Ages: 10–12

Players Needed: 6 or more

Object: To pull the opposing players over the center line

HOW TO PLAY

Before the game, draw a chalk line or lay a rope on the grass to mark the center line. (Make sure the playing area is level and free of debris.) Divide the kids into two teams with an equal number of players who share approximately equal physical strength and weight. Have the players line up in single file on each side of the center line, with a few feet of space between each player. Tie a bandanna or scarf around the middle of the tugging rope and set this marker over the center line.

Each player grabs onto the tugging rope and, on the count of three, tries to pull the first member of the other team over the center line. The game may end right away if the first player on either team steps over the center line—however, it's more likely that all of the players on one team will be pulled across the line and collapse in a giggling pile!

CREATIVE OPTIONS

- Instead of using a line to mark the center, use a big piece of red or brown cloth and call it "hot lava" or "quicksand." The kids will have fun trying to avoid the "dangerous territory."

- Play a second game with only the winners of the previous game. Divide them up into another two teams and start the Tug of War again. When one side wins, divide those winners in half and play again. Continue until there are only two players left to pull on the rope.

- Tie a few sheets together and use them for a rope—it will be easier and softer to hold.

Materials Needed:
- 1 long, sturdy rope (about 8 to 10 feet in length)
- A bandanna or scarf
- A large grassy outdoor area
- Chalk or a long length of rope

PRIZES AND FAVORS

- Give the winning team a big bag of candy to share, and be sure to provide the losers with a fun consolation prize.

- Give the guests fun bandannas to wear at the party or to take home.

- If you use the "dangerous territory" option, give all of the kids books about volcanoes to take home.

TROUBLE-SHOOTING TIPS

- Sometimes the kids get rope burns from the tugging, so choose a smooth rope and ask the players to bring gloves to the party.

- After each round, mix up the team members so the sides aren't lopsided in strength.

- Position bigger kids on the ends of each rope to act as team "anchors."

HA HA HA

In this game, the rules are easy, but the challenge (keeping a straight face) is almost impossible!

For Ages: 6–9

Optional Ages: 10–12

Players Needed: 4 or more

Object: To keep a straight face while the other players try to make you laugh

HOW TO PLAY

The players sit or stand in a circle, and one player begins by saying "Ha," as solemnly as possible. The next player in the circle says, "Ha Ha," and the player after that, "Ha Ha Ha." Play continues with each player adding a "Ha" during his turn. The players must all keep a straight face throughout the game.

Any player who smiles or giggles must leave the circle; however, he can now move around the circle trying to make the other kids laugh. He can make funny faces or noises, but cannot touch the other players. The game ends when only one player remains in the circle by having kept a straight face through all the laughter.

CREATIVE OPTIONS

• Have the players lay on the floor at right angles, with each child's head resting on another's tummy. Once one player's tummy starts shaking from laughter, the other kids will have trouble controlling their giggling!

• Instead of saying "Ha," the kids can say a silly word like "belly button" or "burp." Let the kids choose or make up their own silly words, too.

• Give the kids fake noses or funny hats to wear during the game. It will be harder for everyone to control their impulse to laugh.

Materials Needed:
• Enough space for the players to form a circle

PRIZES AND FAVORS

• Give the kids silly gag gifts to take home—fake noses, joy buzzers, or rubber bugs.

• Offer everyone joke and riddle books to get them laughing again.

• Give the grand prize winner a funny cartoon videotape.

TROUBLE-SHOOTING TIPS

• Make sure the kids who are out don't try to tickle or touch the other players to make them laugh.

• This is a quick game, so play a few rounds or have other activities planned, too.

3-D TIC-TAC-TOE

All kids love the challenge of Tic-Tac-Toe. Here's a 3-D version that they'll want to play again and again.

For Ages: 6–9

Optional Ages: 2–5

Players Needed: 2 or more (2 play at a time)

Object: To be the first player to get three squares in a row—up, down, or diagonally

HOW TO PLAY

In traditional Tic-Tac-Toe, a grid is divided into nine squares, and two players take turns marking an X or an O in the squares. To win, a player must get three of her marks in a row—up, down, or diagonally. If no one gets three in a row, the game is a draw.

The 3-D version takes a little more skill. Before the game, draw a Tic-Tac-Toe grid on the pavement, closing the grid up by connecting all of the unconnected lines (if you can't play outdoors, use masking tape to create a closed-up Tic-Tac-Toe grid on a tile floor). Then collect beanbags (you can buy them at toy and craft stores, or make them yourself by filling old socks with dried beans or rice and tying a knot in the sock tops). Mark three of the bags with X's and three with O's.

At game time, the kids stand several feet away from the grid, and two players begin—one with the X beanbags and one with the O beanbags. They alternate turns tossing the beanbags into the grid, trying to get three of their bags in a row. If a player tosses one of her beanbags away from the grid, she can take another turn—the beanbag *must* land in a square. If her beanbag lands in a square occupied by another player's beanbag, the other beanbag is removed and must be tossed again. The player who gets three in a row first is the winner.

CREATIVE OPTIONS

• Let the kids make the beanbags before the game—just provide the socks and "beans" and show them what to do. (Let each player create three beanbags for her own use during the game.)

• Play a Tic-Tac-Toe variation in which the player who gets three bags in a row first is the *loser.*

• Number the grid squares one to nine and have silly instructions to go with each number: "Jump backwards on one foot," "Bark like a dog," "Make a weird sound without moving your lips," and so on. When the kids toss their beanbags onto the grid, they must do the corresponding action.

PRIZES AND FAVORS

• Let the kids take their beanbags home.

• Fill some homemade beanbags with jelly beans, and let the kids open the beanbags and eat the candy.

• Give all of the winners activity books filled with Tic-Tac-Toe games.

TROUBLE-SHOOTING TIPS

• If any of the kids have trouble with their aim, allow them to stand closer to the grid.

• To avoid boredom and having guests wait for turns, draw several Tic-Tac-Toe grids in your playing area. Have at least one adult supervising the games at each grid.

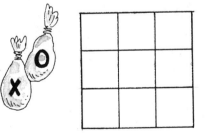

BINGO

Everyone loves to play Bingo! The game preparation takes a few minutes, but the fun is long-lasting, and the cards can be used again and again.

For Ages: 6–9

Optional Ages: 2–5

Players Needed: 3 or more

Object: To be the first player to cover five spaces in a row—up, down, or diagonally

HOW TO PLAY

Before the party, make some Bingo grids on white paper by drawing five squares across each horizontal row and five squares down each vertical row. At the top of each grid write B-I-N-G-O, and fill in the squares by writing any numbers from one to fifty. Each grid should have a random sampling of numbers when you're done. Then make some Bingo caller cards out of different-colored pieces of paper cut into small squares and labeled with the letter/number combinations on the grid—B-21, I-36, N-11, G-50, etc. (all the letter/number combinations must be added to the caller cards).

At game time, you'll play the role of the Caller. Give each player a handful of small tokens to hold on to (try pennies, buttons, or Hershey's Kisses); then mix up the Bingo caller cards, draw one, and announce it to the players. Any player who has a corresponding letter/number combination on his grid, covers the spot with a token. Continue to draw caller cards and announce letters/numbers until one of the players has filled a row with tokens—up, down, or diagonally. That player shouts, "Bingo!" and wins the game.

CREATIVE OPTIONS

• Let the kids take turns being the Caller.

• For a longer game, see which player can fill up an entire grid first.

• Make Bingo grids that have squares filled with different letters of the alphabet and call out letters in a random order. The player who gets five in a row first wins.

Materials Needed:
- Paper (plain white and colored)
- Scissors
- A pencil or pen
- Small tokens (try pennies, buttons, or Hershey's Kisses)
- *Optional:* clear Contact paper

PRIZES AND FAVORS

- Give each player a homemade Bingo grid and playing cards.

- Let the kids take home their tokens.

- Give the big winner a special prize, such as a store-bought Bingo game, a bag of Hershey's Kisses, or a piggy bank.

TROUBLE-SHOOTING TIPS

- If you play more than one round, have the players switch playing cards—you'll be more likely to get a variety of winners.

- Put the Bingo caller cards aside after you draw them so you can check to make sure the player who calls, "Bingo!" has really won.

- Cover the Bingo playing cards with clear Contact paper so they won't get ripped in the excitement.

SLAP, CLAP, AND SNAP

Slap, Clap, and Snap is a classic twist on the traditional game Categories. It takes some coordination and quick thinking, and will keep the kids entertained for a long time.

For Ages: 6–9

Optional Ages: 10–12

Players Needed: 4 or more

Object: To be the last remaining player in the circle

HOW TO PLAY

Have the players sit cross-legged in a circle and choose one player to start. The first player chooses a category like "colors," "names," "foods," "TV shows," or any other one she can think of. Then she begins to slap, clap, and snap in rhythm by slapping her legs twice, clapping twice, and snapping her left fingers and then her right in an even rhythm. All of the other players do the same actions in the same rhythm so that everyone in the circle is slapping, clapping, and snapping at once.

The starting player then calls out an item from the chosen category, saying it just after she snaps, without changing or losing the rhythm. The next player in the circle follows in turn, naming another item in the category just after snapping. Play continues in this manner around the circle and doesn't stop until a player can't think of an item, repeats an item, or misses the beat—that player is out of the game and must leave the circle. The next round begins with a new category. The game is over when only one player remains in the circle—that player is the winner.

CREATIVE OPTIONS

• Play the game without a winner to avoid competition. Just continue the game after a player misses, but start a new category.

• To add some suspense, have each player point to another player to signal that it's her turn, rather than taking turns in a circle. For example, the first player calls out an item while clapping and points to any other player while everyone else is snapping. That player must keep the rhythm, call out an item after snapping, and point to another

Materials Needed:
• Enough space for the players to form a circle

player. It's easier to make a mistake in this version, producing lots of giggles!

• Play an active, outdoor version by having the kids bounce a ball back and forth between players. Each time a player catches the ball, she must name an item in the category and quickly bounce the ball to another player.

PRIZES AND FAVORS

• Give all of the kids cassette singles of popular songs to snap and clap to at home.

• If you play the outdoor version, give the kids sports balls or small, bouncy rubber balls to take with them.

• Give the grand prize winner a board game.

TROUBLE-SHOOTING TIPS

• Have the kids slap, clap, and snap at a slow pace so each player will have a few seconds to come up with a category item. Once everybody gets the hang of it, the pace can speed up.

• Keep a list of simple category suggestions handy in case the players have trouble coming up with any.

MUMMY WRAP

Kids love to act like scary monsters, and this game gives them a chance to do just that. It's also a great icebreaker for kids who don't know each other very well.

For Ages: 6–9

Optional Ages: 10–12

Players Needed: 6 or more

Object: To be the first player to wrap your partner from head to toe like a mummy

HOW TO PLAY

Divide the kids into pairs, with one player as the Mummy and the other as the Mummy Wrapper. On the count of three (after a warning that the toilet paper is "very old and delicate"), all of the Mummy Wrappers must race to wrap their Mummies with the rolls of toilet paper as fast as they can.

To win, a Mummy Wrapper has to be the first to wrap his Mummy from head to toe (except for the face). In the hurry and excitement of wrapping, the players will soon find that the toilet paper will tear, causing all kinds of delays, do-overs, and giggles. To make the mummy wrapping easier, provide tape.

CREATIVE OPTIONS

• Use rolls of crepe paper (available at party supply stores) for a more heavy-duty wrapping. Choose different colors for each "mummy" pair.

• Buy extra rolls of "mummy wrap" and play another round so everyone gets a chance to be "mummified."

• Have a mummy-wrapping contest and award a prize to everyone for fun categories like "freakiest," "silliest," or "most ghoulish." Decorate the party room with fake cobwebs, monster posters, and glow-in-the-dark accessories, and play scary music in the background (all of these materials are available at party supply stores).

Materials Needed:
- 1 roll of white or colorful toilet paper for every two kids (avoid scented brands)
- **Optional:** tape

PRIZES AND FAVORS

- Take Polaroid snapshots of the completed mummies and send everyone home with a fun photo.

- Give the winning pair a roll of gag-gift toilet paper (available at party supply stores).

- Give everyone a scary action figure (preferably a mummy) from a toy store.

- Offer all of the guests tiny pieces of candy in small plastic pill bottles and tell them it's ancient Egyptian candy that's been sealed in an old tomb for centuries. (Be sure to wash out the pill bottles before adding the candy.)

TROUBLE-SHOOTING TIPS

- If the kids don't seem to be making much progress with the wrapping, you might want to provide tape so they can put any ripped toilet paper back together.

- Be sure to tell the kids to wrap only their partner's body, leaving his face uncovered.

PRICE IT RIGHT

This home version of the classic TV game show is a winner! Kids will love the suspense, and best of all, they'll all win a prize.

For Ages: 6–9

Optional Ages: 10–12

Players Needed: 6 or more

Object: To win a prize by guessing closest to its actual price

HOW TO PLAY

Before the party, set out prizes in the party room (make sure the actual prices are covered up). Then make price tags from construction paper, write the prices on them, and fold them over so the prices are hidden. For added fun, write lavish descriptions of each item on the front of the tags.

At game time, the kids must guess the price of each item, secretly writing their answers on pieces of paper. Once everyone has written down the price of the first item, have the kids read their estimates aloud. Then open the price tag and announce the price of the item. The player whose guess is closest to the actual price wins the item and is out of the game. Play continues until all of the gifts are won and everyone has a prize.

CREATIVE OPTIONS

• Allow the kids to hold a gift exchange after the game—they can trade prizes with one another if they want.

• Ask the guests to bring a white elephant gift from home along with the price of the item (they may have to do some research to find out the price). Have the rest of the kids guess the values—whomever guesses closest to the actual price has to keep the item!

• Have the kids pretend they're game show contestants. Provide adult dress-up clothes or ask the kids to come in costume. You can make name tags with funny names, using construction paper, for each guest, too.

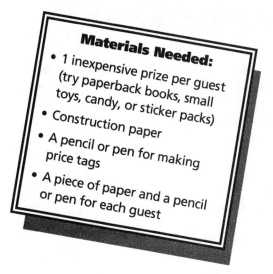

Materials Needed:

- 1 inexpensive prize per guest (try paperback books, small toys, candy, or sticker packs)
- Construction paper
- A pencil or pen for making price tags
- A piece of paper and a pencil or pen for each guest

PRIZES AND FAVORS

- Along with the prizes they've already won, provide a few extra bonus prizes like bubblegum or fun pencils and erasers.

- If you have the kids dress up, let everyone keep an accessory or item of clothing, such as sunglasses or a fun hat.

- Give all of the kids inexpensive calculators to take home. They'll love playing with them during the party, too!

TROUBLE-SHOOTING TIPS

- If there is a tie for a price estimate, have the kids guess a number from one to ten to decide the winner.

- When choosing the prizes, make sure you select generic items that all of the guests will enjoy, especially if there are both girls and boys invited.

PUZZLE HUNT

This fast-paced, silly race is fun for a large or small group. You can make the challenge as easy or difficult as you want, depending on the ages of the guests.

For Ages: 6–9

Optional Ages: 10–12

Players Needed: 4 or more

Object: To be the first to get rid of your puzzle pieces

HOW TO PLAY

Before the game, decide how many pictures and pieces of tagboard you'll need based on the number of guests. Draw puzzle shapes (about the size of a child's palm) with a felt-tip pen over each picture, leaving the middle portions of the pictures intact and a puzzle border around the edges. Then coat the back of each picture with spray adhesive and stick the pictures onto tagboard. When the adhesive has dried, cut out the puzzle pieces along the border. Make sure your homemade puzzle *looks* like a puzzle and that all the pieces will fit together again!

At game time, place the pictures, minus their "puzzle" borders, on flat surfaces around the party room and divide the mixed-up puzzle pieces equally among the guests. On the count

of three, the kids must scramble around to the different puzzle borders to find where their pieces fit. The kids will soon find that they have to cooperate with other players to figure out where their pieces go, even though they're racing against each other—that's part of the fun. The first player to fit her last puzzle piece into a puzzle border before anyone else (whether the puzzle itself is complete or not) is the winner. When you have a winner, let the rest of the guests complete the puzzles.

CREATIVE OPTIONS

• If you have a really large group, allow the kids to work in pairs.

• Photocopy school photos of the guests, have them enlarged at a copy store, and use them as the puzzle pieces.

Materials Needed:
- Large, colorful pictures that you can turn into "puzzles" (posters, coloring book pages, or magazine photos)—1 or 2 pictures per guest
- Large sheets of tagboard—enough to back each picture
- Spray adhesive
- Scissors
- A felt-tip pen

• Make the game more difficult for older kids by cutting out smaller puzzle pieces or using similar pictures (for example, posters of the four Teenage Mutant Ninja Turtles).

PRIZES AND FAVORS

• Give the winner all of the completed puzzles to try the game again at home.

• Give everyone a fun box puzzle.

• Send everyone home with a coloring book or poster.

TROUBLE-SHOOTING TIPS

• Make sure the puzzle pieces are large enough for the kids to handle so they won't get frustrated.

• For a race with less confusion, allow the kids to look at the puzzles and pieces for a few minutes before the game begins.

SWITCH

This is one of those "What's wrong with this picture?" activities that kids are familiar with from school—but this one is much more fun!

For Ages: 6–9

Optional Ages: 2–5

Players Needed: 6 or more

Object: To figure out which guests are wearing the wrong clothes

HOW TO PLAY

Divide the kids into two teams and take the first team into another room. This team must switch various items of clothing (or accessories) with one another so that each team member has traded something she was wearing with another team member. (Tell the kids to switch items like shoes, belts, barrettes, socks, or sweaters—not shirts or pants—and let boys trade items with girls.) If you think the kids will have trouble remembering any accessories that were traded, write them down on a piece of paper. This will prevent confusion when it's time to switch back.

Once the first team has switched clothing, the players return to the party room and the other team must guess what's different. When a player thinks she might know what switch has

been made, she can shout out the answer. If she's right, give her a candy treat. See if the kids can correctly identify all of the "switches" on your list. Then let the second team try to stump the first team.

CREATIVE OPTIONS

- For a bigger challenge, have the team that's guessing identify the items that have been switched *and* the players who did the switching.

- Instead of having the kids switch their own clothes, gather some items of clothing and accessories for the kids to put on over their own outfits (try a pair of socks, a watch, a necklace, a vest, and so on). Let the kids dress up, return to the party room, and try to fool the other team.

Materials Needed:
- A piece of paper and a pencil or pen
- Candy or other treats

- Have the team members switch only their shoes with each other. The other team must guess which shoes belong to whom.

PRIZES AND FAVORS

- Give all of the kids an accessory to wear home such as a pair of funny socks, some costume jewelry, or a silly hat.

- Give everyone a funny dress-up outfit such as a grass hula skirt, an occupational uniform, or a long dress. You can find all sorts of fun and inexpensive clothing at thrift shops. The kids will have a ball wearing these outfits during the party.

- Offer the kids fun jewelry items such as barrettes or surfer bracelets.

TROUBLE-SHOOTING TIPS

- Remind the kids to exchange only outer clothing—nothing embarrassing.

- If the game seems too easy for the guests you're inviting, ask them ahead of time to dress in mismatched clothes with lots of extra accessories.

PUMPING IRON

Here's another great party icebreaker. The kids have to work together to win this fun and silly challenge.

For Ages: 6–9

Optional Ages: 10–12

Players Needed: 4 or more

Object: To stuff the most balloons into your team's "Weakling" to create "muscles"

HOW TO PLAY

This game takes some preparation beforehand, but it's well worth the effort! If you don't want to blow up a bunch of balloons yourself, rent a helium machine or recruit some helpers.

At game time, divide the kids into two teams. Select one guest from each team to be the Weakling—the remaining guests are the Personal Trainers. Have the teams gather on opposite sides of the room and divide the balloons up equally among them. Then have each Weakling put on a union suit (a pair of one-piece long underwear) over his clothes.

On the count of three, the two teams of Personal Trainers must make their Weaklings grow some instant muscles by stuffing as many balloons as possible into the union suits.

Give the teams two minutes on a timer to do this. When the time is up, let everyone admire the Weaklings' new muscles (be sure to have a camera ready!). Then remove the balloons from the union suits one at a time, counting as you go. The team that stuffed the most balloons wins, but popped balloons don't count toward the total.

CREATIVE OPTIONS

- Buy or borrow union suits for half of the guests and divide the kids into partners instead of teams. After one pair has won, let the kids switch roles so they each get a turn posing and stuffing (you'll need extra balloons for this option).

- Instead of having a race, let the kids stuff one Weakling to see how many balloons they can use up. If you have enough balloons, let everyone take a turn getting stuffed.

Materials Needed:
- About 50–100 small inflated balloons
- 2 adult-size union suits (one-piece long underwear)
- A timer

PRIZES AND FAVORS

• Send everyone home with a poster of Arnold Schwarzenegger as the "Terminator."

• Give the guests books or activity booklets about exercise.

• Hand out helium or Mylar balloons to all of the kids.

TROUBLE-SHOOTING TIPS

• Use small balloons (or don't inflate the balloons very much) because you want the kids to be able to stuff them into the union suits easily.

• Make sure to pick up all of the balloon pieces after the game—they can be dangerous around small children and animals.

TONGUE TEASERS

Have a camera ready for this game—you're sure to get some great photos of funny faces!

For Ages: 6–9

Optional Ages: 10–12

Players Needed: 4 or more

Object: To identify the most "mystery" foods by tasting them

HOW TO PLAY

Place some mystery foods in separate bowls and add serving spoons. Then write the numbers one through eight clockwise on paper plates (one number for each food item). Pass out the paper plates and spoons to the guests. Have the kids sit in a circle so they will be able to see each other's expressions.

At game time, put a dab of the first food by the first number on each player's plate. Once everyone is served, the kids must taste the mystery food and secretly write down what they think it is on pieces of paper. (Wait until you see their expressions!) Repeat these steps for every food item. At the end of the taste tests, see which guest got the most correct answers—that player wins.

CREATIVE OPTIONS

- For younger kids, allow everyone to shout out what they think the mystery food is (after everyone has tasted it) rather than writing the answers down.

- Tint the mystery foods with food coloring to disguise them a little.

- Play the tasting game with breakfast cereals. Buy a variety pack of cereals, pour them into small brown paper lunch bags so the kids can't see them, and have the kids sample them one by one and try to guess the brand.

- With a more adventurous group of kids, use food items that are difficult to identify, such as mashed garbanzo beans or pureed vegetables.

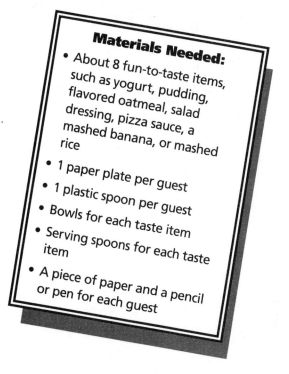

Materials Needed:
- About 8 fun-to-taste items, such as yogurt, pudding, flavored oatmeal, salad dressing, pizza sauce, a mashed banana, or mashed rice

- 1 paper plate per guest
- 1 plastic spoon per guest
- Bowls for each taste item
- Serving spoons for each taste item
- A piece of paper and a pencil or pen for each guest

PRIZES AND FAVORS

- Give all of the kids mini boxes of cereal from variety packs.

- Send everyone home with a mystery food, such as a few homemade cookies or an unwrapped candy bar sealed in aluminum foil and tied with a ribbon.

- Give the grand prize winner a kids' cook-book, a fast food gift certificate collection, or a book of kids' mysteries.

TROUBLE-SHOOTING TIPS

- When selecting food items, avoid foods that are tart or that kids don't like.

- If a player seems hesitant about tasting anything, let her watch the other players first. She may want to join in later when she sees it's fun to play.

THE INVISIBLE GIFT

This game is a fun combination of Telephone, Gossip, and Charades. It's a good noncompetitive activity for an indoor party.

For Ages: 6–9

Optional Ages: 10–12

Players Needed: 6 or more

Object: To identify the "invisible" item

HOW TO PLAY

The players form a circle—they can sit or stand. The first player secretly thinks of an object such as a toy, an animal, or a food item and must pretend to handle it and pass it to the next player in the circle. For instance, if he has chosen a cat for his object, he could pretend to scoop it up, hold it, kiss it, pet it, and feed it a can of cat food. He must do all of this without talking and then hand the mysterious item to the next person.

The next player must pretend to take the item, indicate what it is without talking, and pass it to the next player. Play continues around the circle until the last player receives the item. The last player announces to the group what he thinks the item is. If he's wrong, the second-to-last player can take a guess. If that player is also wrong, the third-to-last player gets a guess, and so on, until someone gets the correct answer. If no one gets the answer right, the first player reveals what the intended object was. Play a new round, so a new player can choose the object.

CREATIVE OPTIONS

• Instead of having the kids try to think of an object, fill a bag with all sorts of items and have each player secretly choose one when it's his turn to act. (Remove the items after each round so they won't be chosen twice.)

• After the kids have played the game using objects, have them demonstrate a whole invisible activity, such as eating breakfast or taking a shower.

Materials Needed:
• Enough space for the players to form a wide circle

• For a fun twist, have all of the players close their eyes while the demonstration is going on *except* for the player who's acting and the one who's going to relay the information. The guesses should be pretty funny by the end of the game!

PRIZES AND FAVORS

• Send everyone home with a mystery present wrapped in gift wrap or hidden in a small brown paper lunch bag.

• If you choose to do the option with the bag full of goodies, fill it with fun items for kids. After each player has chosen one, let him keep it.

• Give everyone mystery books or pads of paper and "invisible ink" pens.

TROUBLE-SHOOTING TIP

• If the kids have trouble thinking up items that are easy to describe with actions only, make a list of appropriate items and whisper one to each player when it's his turn. Include simple, concrete items, such as a scarf, book, plant, ball, or can of soda.

TICKET, PLEASE

This fun game takes quick thinking. You'll find that it's a good indoor game for an active group of kids.

For Ages: 6–9

Optional Ages: 2–5

Players Needed: 7 or more

Object: To travel from one spot to another safely

HOW TO PLAY

Arrange some chairs in a circle facing inward, with enough room in the center of the circle for the kids to run around in. Choose one player to be the Conductor. The Conductor stands in the middle of the circle.

Mix up postcards and pass them out to every player but the Conductor. Tell the players to keep their destinations (the places featured on the postcards) a secret. Then give the Conductor a list of the destinations indicated on the postcards, as well as a few that aren't (prepare this list before the game). The Conductor calls out one of the destinations on the list, and the two players holding the postcards that match the destination must jump up and switch places *before* the Conductor can take one of their empty seats. If the Conduc-

tor reaches an empty chair first, the player who's left standing becomes the Conductor.

CREATIVE OPTIONS

• For younger kids, use pictures of zoo animals instead of places, and call the Conductor the Zookeeper. Provide the Zookeeper with a list of animal stickers so she can glance at those instead of trying to read words.

• For older kids, choose postcards with similar-sounding destinations so they have to listen carefully, or just add similar-sounding places to the Conductor's list (Iowa, Idaho, Ohio, Hawaii, etc.).

• Have the Conductor sit in the circle rather than stand so she has to quickly scramble for an empty seat.

Materials Needed:

- Chairs for all but one player
- Enough space for all of the kids to form a wide circle
- Pairs of identical postcards featuring different destinations—enough for all but one player (for instance, 6 postcards for 7 players, with 2 of Disneyland, 2 of London, and 2 of Rome)
- A piece of paper and a pencil or pen

PRIZES AND FAVORS

- Send the world travelers home with posters of foreign countries or maps of the world.

- Give the kids souvenirs like British candy or Chinese puzzles.

- Offer everyone fun postcards, stamped and ready to send to a friend or relative.

- If you try the option for younger kids, send everyone home with stickers featuring zoo animals.

TROUBLE-SHOOTING TIPS

- Spread the chairs out in a wide circle so there's plenty of room. That way there's less risk of the kids crashing into each other.

- If the Conductors always find a seat first and seem unchallenged, have them close their eyes while calling out destinations and open them when they hear the other players scrambling for chairs.

ALPHABET GAME SHOW

This quick-paced quiz game will keep the kids on their toes. They'll want to play it over and over.

For Ages: 6–9

Optional Ages: 10–12

Players Needed: 4 or more

Object: To be the first player to name items in categories and win the most alphabet cards

HOW TO PLAY

Before the game, write each letter of the alphabet on a separate index card. Then think up fun categories that kids can relate to (animals, names, TV shows, sports and hobbies, cartoon characters, etc.) and write each one separately on index cards. Next, put the alphabet cards in a separate pile from the category cards and shuffle both piles.

At game time, choose one player to be the Game Show Host. He must pick a card from the category pile and hold it up for all of the other players to see. He then chooses an alphabet card, holds it up for everyone to see, and announces the letter. The first player to name an item in the category that begins with the alphabet letter wins the card. For instance, if the host chooses candy bars as a category

and pulls the letter M from the pile, the first player to call out, "Milky Way," or, "Mounds," wins the alphabet card. At that time, you can choose another Game Show Host or let the same one choose another two cards. The player with the most alphabet cards at the end of the game is the winner.

CREATIVE OPTIONS

- If you want to have a noncompetitive game, just omit the part where the kids keep the alphabet cards. Instead, shuffle the alphabet cards back into the pile and continue.

- Let the kids think up their own categories instead of making the cards ahead of time.

- For a more challenging version of the game, make up Bingo grids with five squares across and five squares down. Write the same five

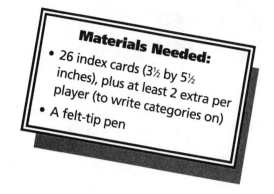

Materials Needed:
- 26 index cards (3½ by 5½ inches), plus at least 2 extra per player (to write categories on)
- A felt-tip pen

categories by each square on the left side of the grids and five different alphabet letters by the squares at the top of the grids. To play, the players must fill in the squares of the grids, matching categories with alphabet letters as quickly as possible (set a two-minute time limit). After time has been called, have the players read off their answers for each letter.

PRIZES AND FAVORS

- Send the kids home with items that relate to the categories, such as comic books if the category is cartoon characters or giant Hershey bars if the category is candy bars.

- Give the winner the board game "Scatter-gories."

TROUBLE-SHOOTING TIPS

- To make the game go more smoothly, you can omit letters that are especially difficult such as Q, X, and Z.

- You can also allow the kids to use the difficult letters *within* a word, rather than at the beginning of the word.

MYSTERY MASTERPIECE

The kids will love the surprise result of this activity. And it's so easy, they'll be able to try it at home again after the party!

For Ages: 6–9

Optional Ages: 10–12

Players Needed: Groups of 4

Object: To create a crazy creature one part at a time

WHAT TO DO

Before the activity, divide pieces of paper into four panels by folding each one over from the short edge three times. Or demonstrate to the kids how it's done and let them do the folding themselves. Seat the kids around a table.

Have each child draw the head of a favorite animal, person, or creature in the top panel with felt-tip pens, making the neck extend into a small portion of the second panel. (For added fun, suggest that the kids try to draw the body parts of cartoon characters, space creatures, robots, or monsters.) They should then fold the paper over so that the head isn't visible but the bottom of the neck is. After that, they must pass the folded piece of paper to the child on their right who adds a body and arms in the second panel, beginning with

the neck and ending with the waistline. (The kids must not peek at the previous drawing!) Tell the kids to extend the creature's waistline below the panel, and pass the folded piece of paper to the right. The third panel of each piece of paper will feature legs, and the last panel will have the feet. When the drawings are complete, the kids can unfold their "masterpieces" and share them with the rest of the group. The results will be some crazy creatures and lots of laughter!

CREATIVE OPTIONS

- Divide the paper into six panels for extra fun. The first panel can feature the top of the head, eyes, and nose; the second panel, the face, mouth, chin, and neck; the third panel, the upper torso and arms; the fourth panel, the lower torso; the fifth panel, the legs; and the sixth, the feet.

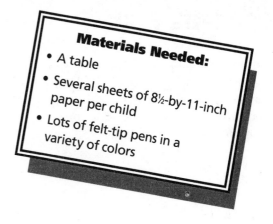

Materials Needed:
- A table
- Several sheets of 8½-by-11-inch paper per child
- Lots of felt-tip pens in a variety of colors

- The kids can cut the body parts out and swap them to create even more silly combinations. Give them tape to hold the creatures together.

- Provide art supplies such as paint, crayons, glitter, and glue so the kids can really go wild with the drawings.

PRIZES AND FAVORS

- Let each of the kids keep a completed picture. Before sending the pictures home with the kids, glue them to posterboard and write the names of the artists near the different body parts.

- Give the kids felt-tip pens, pads of paper, paint sets, or other art supplies.

TROUBLE-SHOOTING TIP

- If the kids worry about not being good at art, tell them it's not a contest and that the pictures are supposed to look silly anyway.

PUPPET FUN

Kids love to make things that they can use over and over—a puppet-making party will give them this opportunity. And they're easy to make using the simplest household materials!

For Ages: 6–9

Optional Ages: 2–5

Players Needed: Any group size

Object: To create reusable puppets

WHAT TO DO

Set up the art materials at a table—this will make it easier for the kids to work on their projects. The kids can start by making puppet bodies using socks, bags, cups, or wooden spoons.

For a paper bag puppet, have the kids draw the eyes and nose over the bag's bottom flap—the underside of the flap becomes the mouth. Let the kids use glitter, ribbons, and yarn to give the puppets some sparkle and flair. For a wooden spoon puppet, the kids can simply create a face on the spoon part, using felt-tip pens, and hold the handle to control the puppet's movement. They can make fun soft puppets with socks, simply adding buttons or pom-poms for eyes. To make a small paper cup puppet, just have the kids cut two holes

below the cup rim, turn the cup upside down, and insert two fingers in the holes for crazy puppet legs—a face and decorations can be added with crayons and other art supplies.

When the puppet-making activity is finished, give the kids some time to come up with a script, and put on a puppet show for the parents (have them pick the kids up twenty minutes early and enjoy the production).

CREATIVE OPTIONS

• Make some awards for the kids, using fun categories such as "silliest-looking puppet," "most decorative," or "funniest puppet voice." Make sure to pick out something special about *each* project so every child will feel special.

Materials Needed:
- A table
- Socks
- Wooden spoons
- Small paper cups
- Brown paper grocery bags or small brown paper lunch bags
- Glue
- Children's scissors
- Buttons and/or pom-poms
- Ribbons and yarn
- Glitter
- Felt-tip pens and/or crayons (assorted colors)

- Have the kids make a simple puppet stage by spreading sheets over the table. They can hide behind it for their puppet show.

- Write a funny puppet show script before the party, with a part for each guest's puppet. Have the kids learn their parts, or provide photocopies of the scripts so everyone can follow along.

PRIZES AND FAVORS

- Let the kids keep their puppets.

- Give everyone a collection of puppet supplies for creative puppet-making at home.

- Offer books that teach kids how to make more advanced puppets.

TROUBLE-SHOOTING TIPS

- Ask adult volunteers to help with the puppet-making activity. This will prevent the kids from getting confused or frustrated waiting for help.

- If the kids worry about not being good at art, tell them it's not a contest and that the puppets should look silly or fun anyway.

FACE PAINTING

Face painting has become a popular activity with kids of all ages. It's an especially fun activity for a party because the kids will have a place to show off the decorations.

For Ages: 6–9

Optional Ages: 2–5, 10–12

Players Needed: Any group size

Object: To create fun artwork on your partner

WHAT TO DO

Before the activity, gather all of the face-painting materials—pens, paper, and mirrors—and put them on the table. Then make awards out of construction paper for categories such as "most creative," "funniest," or "best use of color"—one for each guest.

Divide the kids into pairs or let them choose partners for face painting. This activity works best if the kids sketch some designs first, so let them take their time experimenting on paper. When they're ready, have the artists begin painting their partners' cheeks, avoiding the eye and mouth area. If you prefer to use accessories like make-up and stickers, let the kids use the stickers for a basic design and paint colorful scenes around them. Or let them freely experiment with color, using the stickers for body designs. When they're done painting, allow their partners to admire their new faces in the mirror for a while, and let the artists show off their work to everyone. Then have the partners try their hand at face painting. The kids won't want to stop there! Let them paint designs on their hands or use partners again. Give everybody a special award at the end.

CREATIVE OPTIONS

• Buy packages of temporary tattoos (available at discount and toy stores) and let the kids go crazy putting tattoos all over each other's bodies—on their ankles, arms, wrists, and tummies.

• Give the artists specific themes to create, such as monsters, flowers, or animals, and

Materials Needed:
- A table
- Face paints (available at craft, party supply, toy, and art supply stores)
- *Or* face-painting accessories, such as lipstick, eye shadow, "clown white" make-up, (available at costume shops or drugstores), and stickers
- White paper
- Felt-tip pens
- Mirrors
- Construction paper

have the rest of the group guess what the artist has painted.

- Have a jar of cold cream and a box of tissues on hand so the kids can clean up and do the activity again with different partners. Take Polaroid snapshots of each design before cleanup, if possible.

PRIZES AND FAVORS

- Give the kids several tubes of face paint to take home.

- Offer everyone fun stickers and temporary tattoos to use at the party or take home.

- Send everyone home with their awards and Polaroid snapshots.

TROUBLE-SHOOTING TIPS

- If freehand painting is too difficult for the kids, provide picture books or magazines and let the kids copy designs of their choice.

- If the kids worry about not being good at art, tell them it's not a contest and that the goal is just to have fun.

- Provide the kids with old T-shirts to protect their clothing.

WATER FROLIC

You don't need a swimming pool to have a water frolic. Here are some fun ways for the kids to beat the heat, get wet, and stay entertained for hours.

For Ages: 6–9

Optional Ages: 2–5, 10–12

Players Needed: Any group size

Object: To stay cool and entertained for hours

WHAT TO DO

Specify on the invitations that the guests bring bathing suits and towels to the party. Then set up one area of the lawn for a water war, one for sprinklers and hoses, and one for a water slide. For the water war, you'll need squirt guns, basters, squirt bottles, plastic pails, and sponges. Set up the hose and sprinkler in another area (if possible, poke holes in an old garden hose so there's lots of spray to run through). Make a slippery water slide by cutting several large plastic garbage bags open to form long rectangles and taping them together with waterproof tape. Place the "slide" on the lawn (preferably on a gentle incline). If you prefer not to make a slide, you can buy one at a toy or discount store. Set a hose at one end to create a rush of water.

At party time, let the kids start off with a water war. Divide them into teams and when you say "Go!" they can squirt the water guns, throw the sponges, or even haul around the pails full of water to get their opponents soaking wet. They can also try squirting party hats off each other's heads with squirt guns (remove the elastic bands from the hats beforehand and tell them *not* to aim for the face). Next, let the kids give the water slide a try. To prevent long lines at the slide, divide the kids into teams again and have one team play in the sprinkler and the other on the slide. Switch after fifteen minutes. The kids should be tired out by the end of the day!

CREATIVE OPTIONS

• During the water war, have the kids try to capture an object sitting in the middle of the other team's territory (the object

Materials Needed:
- A lawn or grassy area
- A hose or sprinkler
- Plastic pails
- Squirt guns
- Basters
- Squirt bottles
- Sponges
- Several large plastic garbage bags
- Scissors
- Waterproof tape
- Party hats

shouldn't be held by anyone). The player who's brave enough to make a mad dash toward the object will get soaked by the other team.

- Make a "water snake" by holding the spout of the hose and moving it back and forth along the ground. Have the kids try to run across the area without getting touched by the water snake.

- The kids can play Follow the Leader down the water slide, with the leader doing a different approach each time. They might slide backwards, face first, or on their knees. Switch leaders after each turn.

PRIZES AND FAVORS

- Give all of the kids a pair of swimming goggles to wear during the party.

- Hand out squirt guns or other water toys.

- Give everyone plastic water bottles featuring fun designs (available at sports stores).

TROUBLE-SHOOTING TIPS

- Supervise the water play to make sure it doesn't get too rough—make sure the kids don't aim for anyone's face during the water war and tell them that only *one* child can be on the water slide at a time.

- Provide sunscreen for all of the kids and encourage them to apply it frequently.

- If the water slide rips, repair it with some waterproof tape. Keep a few extra garbage bags on hand so you can replace torn parts.

- Clear the entire area of any debris so the kids won't get hurt, and warn them to avoid running on wet, slippery grass.

SUPER SUNDAES

Delicious desserts are always a kid-pleaser—especially when *they* get to make them!

For Ages: 6–9

Optional Ages: 10–12

Players Needed: Any group size

Object: To create a yummy treat!

WHAT TO DO

At party time, set the ingredients, bowls, and spoons out on the table and let the kids go to work making their own ice cream sundaes. Tell them that they can make the sundaes as big or as small as they want, but that they need to eat every bite. (Don't actually force the kids to eat until they're too full—you just want to make sure that they don't build a mountain of ice cream.) If you want to make homemade ice cream, let everyone participate. Read the instructions aloud, perform the steps, and get the ice cream maker turning.

For added fun, let the kids do a taste test of each sundae and judge for themselves which one is the yummiest (provide everyone with a tasting bowl and serve a dab of each sundae in the bowls, to prevent spreading germs).

After that, pass out awards made from construction paper to all of the kids for categories such as "tallest sundae," "most creative," or "best use of whipped cream."

CREATIVE OPTIONS

- Instead of making sundaes, give the kids cones and let them make ice cream clowns. The cones can serve as clown hats on top of a round scoop of ice cream. Have the kids create clown faces using the sundae ingredients. Line the clowns up on a cookie sheet and take a picture.

- Let the kids make ice cream caterpillars. Give each child three scoops of ice cream in a row (the caterpillar body) and let them use peppermint sticks for the antennae. Using the sundae ingredients, they can add the eyes, nose, and any other features.

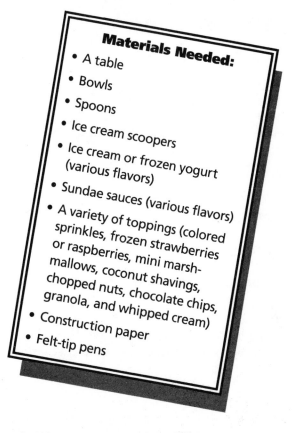

Materials Needed:
- A table
- Bowls
- Spoons
- Ice cream scoopers
- Ice cream or frozen yogurt (various flavors)
- Sundae sauces (various flavors)
- A variety of toppings (colored sprinkles, frozen strawberries or raspberries, mini marshmallows, coconut shavings, chopped nuts, chocolate chips, granola, and whipped cream)
- Construction paper
- Felt-tip pens

- Buy a bunch of bananas and let the kids make banana splits. Just cut the bananas lengthwise, lay the halves in a dish, and place scoops of vanilla, chocolate, and strawberry ice cream on top. The kids can add any sauces or other ingredients.

PRIZES AND FAVORS

- Give everyone gift certificates for treats at an ice cream or yogurt shop.

- Send all of the kids home with ice cream cones filled with small candies and treats.

- Offer the kids small containers of ice cream or cool pops to eat at home.

TROUBLE-SHOOTING TIPS

- Warn the kids not to nibble while creating the sundaes or to eat too much too fast—you don't want anyone to go home with a tummyache.

- Tell the kids to wear old clothes to the party if you're worried about chocolate or other food stains. Or provide old shirts so they won't wear any ice cream home.

- Tell the kids to work quickly—ice cream melts fast!

DAY AT THE BALLPARK

Baseball is an American favorite, so why not treat the kids to a day at the ballpark? Here's an easy party that you can adapt to almost any sporting event.

For Ages: 6–9

Optional Ages: 10–12

Preparation: Purchase the tickets ahead of time and be sure to ask if group rates are available. Inquire about special kids' party activities, too, such as player signings, locker room tours, or getting the guests' names on the scoreboard.

WHAT TO DO

Before the party, have the guests create a team banner, using a large sheet of paper and felt-tip pens. They can hold it up every time their team scores or makes a good play.

Ask all of the guests to wear clothing in the favored team's colors and to bring along their baseballs, mitts, caps, or team pennants. Keep the kids entertained during the ride to the ballpark by giving them each a pack of baseball cards and leading them in a few rounds of "Take Me Out to the Ball Game." (If you've arranged special activities such as a tour of the locker room or autograph signings, you'll need to arrive at the park early.)

During the game, keep a betting pool going, with penny or treat bets on who will hit the

first home run, who will steal a base, or even which food vendor will come by first (record the kids' answers on paper to keep track). Then hand out a penny or treat to each guest who wins a bet. Baseball games usually last a few hours, so be sure to bring some snacks or offer to buy hot dogs and sodas.

CREATIVE OPTIONS

• Buy "ballpark" food (hot dogs, hamburgers, peanuts, and soda) and take along a hibachi for a tailgate party in the parking lot. While the hot dogs are cooking, let the kids toss around a baseball in a safe area.

• Make up a list of baseball trivia questions to ask during the car ride to the park or during the game. Award stickers or bubblegum to the guests who get the right answers first.

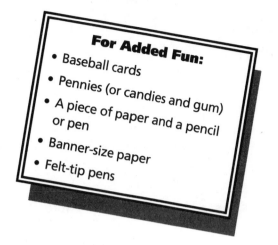

For Added Fun:
- Baseball cards
- Pennies (or candies and gum)
- A piece of paper and a pencil or pen
- Banner-size paper
- Felt-tip pens

- If you don't have a ballpark near your home, host the party around another sport, such as football, basketball, or hockey. Or go to an unusual sporting event, such as a wrestling match or a high school activity.

PRIZES AND FAVORS

- Send the guests home with inexpensive baseball theme items such as stickers, key chains, or erasers.

- Send the kids off with a big bag of fresh peanuts in the shell.

- Give the trivia star a glove, cap, or bat, signed by all of the party guests.

TROUBLE-SHOOTING TIPS

- Find adult volunteers to join you on the trip because the kids will need to go to the bathroom and shouldn't go alone. If you can't round up any volunteers, arrange for a trusted babysitter to come along.

- Use the buddy system on the outing—have the kids choose partners so they'll stay together.

- If the game gets rained out at the last minute, rent a movie about baseball, and keep the kids happy with lots of ballpark food. (Indoor sporting events like basketball, hockey, swimming, and wrestling will not be affected by cold or wet weather.)

OUTDOOR OVERNIGHT

Camping in the great outdoors is an activity kids can't resist. With a little planning, an outdoor overnight can be a great adventure, even if it's just in the backyard.

For Ages: 6–9 (best for more mature six-year-olds)

Optional Ages: 10–12

Preparation: Get out the tent, camping cookware, flashlights, and sleeping bags (you can rent or borrow these items if you don't own them). You'll also need materials for making a camp fire (or use a grill), plus fun food for dinner and breakfast.

WHAT TO DO

Ask the guests to bring along any clothes and gear (don't forget toothbrushes!) needed for overnight camping. Before they arrive, set up the tents, camp fire, and sleeping bags, and have all of the food items ready to go. Or, wait till the kids get there, and make setting up camp a featured activity.

While it's still light out, have a Scavenger Hunt. Divide the kids into two teams and provide each team with a list of items to find outdoors, including both easy- and hard-to-find items (for instance, a white flower, three pine cones, a gray stone, etc.). The team that finds all of the items first wins.

When the sun goes down, serve food cooked on the camp fire or grill, and roast marshmallows for dessert. For before-bed fun, read a few ghost stories and pass around plastic bags full of "body parts"—cooked noodle "guts," eyeballs made from grapes or olives, a Jell–O liver, and a shriveled finger that's really just a raw carrot. Have the kids feel inside the bags to get really grossed-out. When everyone's good and scared, have the kids read comic books by flashlight and tell jokes and riddles so that they won't be too scared to sleep. Let everyone wake up to eggs frying over the fire, or pass out mini boxes of cereal.

CREATIVE OPTIONS

• Have an outdoor "Blind Walk" where some of the kids hold hands and walk around the yard with the guidance of their "sighted leaders." Tell the guides to be careful so no one trips. This activity will help the kids appreciate the sounds and smells of the outdoors a little more.

For Added Fun:
- Food items (grapes or olives, cooked noodles, carrots, and Jell–O)
- Zip-lock plastic sandwich bags
- Paper and a pencil or pen
- A book of ghost stories
- Comic books

- Show the kids how to make shadow figures on the tent walls, using flashlights.

- Give each guest a turn to read a ghost story or make one up.

PRIZES AND FAVORS

- Give the kids packages of freeze-dried food to snack on all night (available at camping and sporting goods stores).

- Give the kids toy compasses, mini flashlights, or plastic magnifying glasses for studying bugs and leaves.

- Give the kids on the team that wins the Scavenger Hunt a few joke books, and give the other kids consolation prizes.

TROUBLE-SHOOTING TIPS

- Some kids might feel afraid to spend a whole night away from home or sleep outdoors. Be sure to camp out with them so they'll feel more confident.

- The party doesn't have to end if it suddenly rains or gets too cold. Be prepared to move indoors if bad weather hits. If the kids are dressed warmly and tents are covered properly with waterproof slicks, however, there's no reason for the fun to go indoors!

- Depending on the size of the group, you might want to ask other adults to spend the night, too. If you can't round up any volunteers, arrange for a trusted babysitter to come over.

STARSHIP TO THE PLANETARIUM

All kids are interested in the mysteries of outer space. A trip to the planetarium can be a cosmic celebration!

For Ages: 6–9

Optional Ages: 10–12

Preparation: Contact a nearby planetarium—they're usually located in a science museum or at a college or university. Call ahead of time to learn the hours of operation, costs, directions, and whether group rates are available.

WHAT TO DO

Before the party, ask all of the guests to bring a plain white T-shirt that can be painted. Pull each shirt over a sheet of cardboard and use thumbtacks to hold the shirts down. Then give the kids paintbrushes and let them go wild painting designs on their shirts with glow-in-the-dark paint. While the paint is drying, let the kids stick glow-in-the-dark stickers all over the shirts for a special effect.

You can also keep the kids busy with a fun activity called "Draw in the Dark." Give the guests a piece of paper and a pencil and have them draw a simple design, such as a star or the sun. Then turn off the lights (you'll need a dark room) and tell the kids to draw the same design. They'll be surprised by the results!

When the shirts are dry, let the kids wear them to the planetarium. They'll shine in the dark as they watch the show. Keep the kids entertained on the ride back home with paperbacks or comic books about outer space. Or bring along the horoscope section from the newspaper and have the guest of honor read all of the fortunes aloud.

CREATIVE OPTIONS

- Before or after the planetarium show, create a spectacular at-home planetarium and surprise the party's guest of honor at the same time. Secretly place a bunch of glow-in-the-dark star stickers on the ceiling of the honoree's bedroom. Gather the guests in the bedroom, turn out the lights, and surprise everyone. Be sure to have the kids wear their glow-in-the-dark shirts!

For Added Fun:
- Glow-in-the-dark paint (available at art, hobby, and paint stores)
- Paintbrushes
- Glow-in-the-dark star stickers (available at science and nature shops or toy stores)
- Cardboard
- Thumbtacks
- Paper and a pencil for each child

• Give each guest a package of freeze-dried astronaut food (ice cream is best) to eat before or after the show (available at camping and sporting goods stores).

PRIZES AND FAVORS

• Send the kids home with their decorated T-shirts and glow-in-the-dark stars.

• Offer books about the stars and planets or wall charts of the galaxy.

TROUBLE-SHOOTING TIPS

• When the kids are painting their shirts, make sure they don't apply the paint too thickly, or the shirts won't dry in time for the show. If the paint hasn't dried in time, place the shirts outside in the sunlight for a few minutes, or use a hair dryer to dry them.

• Remind the kids to be quiet at the planetarium so they won't disturb others.

• Depending on the size of the group, you might want to ask other adults to accompany you. If you can't round up any volunteers, arrange for a trusted babysitter to come along.

TAKEOFF TO THE AIRPORT

The airport offers an afternoon of exciting sights and activities for all ages. If you've got a future pilot in the family, turn this fascination for flight into an airport adventure.

For Ages: 6–9

Optional Ages: 2–5, 10–12

Preparation: Contact your local airport (large or small) to arrange for a tour of the airplanes, control tower, and other facilities. Or, if the weather permits, plan to just have a picnic on the grass in an area by the airport where the planes fly overhead.

WHAT TO DO

The best way to plan an airport outing is to make a preliminary trip to the airport to see what kind of arrangements they have for kids' tours. Find out if it's possible to look inside an airplane, meet a few pilots, see the control tower, go up on the observation deck, or go behind-the-scenes at the baggage claim area. If you can do just one or all of the activities, it's worth it.

Before leaving for the airport, give the guests skycaps and wing pins, and tell them they've just been appointed as pilots and flight attendants. Take an airport transportation bus to the airport, if you can afford the extra cost. If the group is too large for this, drive the kids in your own "airport limo" with posterboard signs that read: "(Your last name) Airlines—

First Class." Have the kids decorate the signs with pictures of airplanes.

When you arrive at the airport, tour the facility as arranged, and then watch some planes take off. If you're planning to have a picnic on the grass instead, pack a basketful of "airline food"—small bags of peanuts, cans of soda, and sandwiches and coleslaw (or potato salad) wrapped in plastic, with plastic silverware on the side. Buy an airplane-shaped cookie cutter and press it on the sandwiches for airplane-shaped sandwiches. Give the kids balsa wood airplanes to assemble and play with outside.

CREATIVE OPTIONS

• Set up a mini-airport at home to greet the guests. Give them their skycaps and wing pins, and usher them into your baggage

For Added Fun:
- Wing pins and skycaps for each child (available at party supply stores and airport gift shops)
- Balsa wood airplanes for each child (available at toy stores)
- Posterboard
- Felt-tip pens

claim area to exchange their party gifts for a baggage claim check (made from construction paper). Have them wait in the "departure room" for the flight call, and draw names to see who gets to be the pilot and sit up in the "cockpit" (the front seat of the car). Everyone else will be flight attendants or passengers. Provide fun dress-up clothes, for added fun.

- If there's some extra time, play Airplane (see p. 84 for directions).

PRIZES AND FAVORS

- Send the kids home with their balsa wood airplanes, wing pins, and skycaps.

- Let each child pick out one inexpensive item from the airport gift shop.

- Offer everyone small toy airplanes.

TROUBLE-SHOOTING TIPS

- Keep a close eye on each child—airports are big, crowded places, and you don't want anyone to get lost. Provide name tags for all of the guests, with the address and phone number of the party host—just in case!

- Find adult volunteers to join you on the trip because the kids might be tempted to run around in all that open space. If you can't round up any volunteers, arrange for a trusted babysitter to come along.

KITES AT THE PARK

You don't need a gusty day to have a kite-flying party at the park—a little breeze will give your kites and kite-flyers a lift.

For Ages: 6–9

Optional Ages 2–5

Preparation: Look in the Yellow Pages under "Kites" for kite stores, and purchase ready-made kites. You can also find kites in hobby and craft stores. Find a park that's free of trees and telephone poles.

WHAT TO DO

If you plan to fly store-bought kites, you can still do a kite-making activity before you head to the park. Gather art materials together and give each child a small brown paper lunch bag. Begin demonstrating the following steps, pausing often to check that the kids are following directions properly: (1) Fold the open edge of each bag back approximately one and a half inches, (2) Tape a piece of string about five inches long to each corner of the open end of the bags, and join these strings with a knot, (3) Add a long piece of string (about five feet) to each knot. (The bags should fly when the kids hold the strings and run.) For some really fun kites, have the kids decorate the paper bags using felt-tip pens, glitter, and stickers.

When you get to the park, tell the kids to, "Go fly a kite!" After all that running around, the kids will be hungry, so pack a picnic basket and spread the lunch out on a picnic table or on the grass. Take along sandwiches cut into diamond shapes and decorated to look like kites—dip a toothpick in food coloring and paint lines on the bread.

CREATIVE OPTIONS

• Before the outing, play a game of Pin the Tail on the Kite. Draw a picture of a tailless kite and give construction paper tails to the kids. Play using the rules of Pin the Tail on the Donkey (see p. 4 for directions).

• Have a kite contest with lots of prizes for "craziest kite," "funniest kite-flying technique," "most likely to get off the ground," or other silly categories.

For Added Fun:
- Small brown paper lunch bags
- Felt-tip pens
- Tape
- String
- Glitter
- Stickers
- Glue
- Toothpicks
- Food coloring
- Diamond-shaped cookie cutter

- Bring along other gadgets that are guaranteed to stay airborne, such as Frisbees, parachute toys, and boomerangs, in case the kites don't fly as planned.

PRIZES AND FAVORS

- Let the kids keep their kites and give everyone an extra ball of string.

- Offer everyone their own pack of felt-tip pens for the kite-decorating activity.

- Give the winner of Pin the Tail on the Kite a book on kite-making.

TROUBLE-SHOOTING TIPS

- Bring at least one "reserve" kite along, in case a child's kite rips or blows away.

- It's probably necessary to have an adult volunteer to help the kids make their kites.

That way, the kids won't get bored or frustrated waiting for help.

- Find adult volunteers to join you on the trip because the kids will want to run off in different directions outside. If you can't round up any volunteers, arrange for a trusted babysitter to come along.

ABRACADABRA— A MAGICIAN!

All kids love magic and have dreamed of being a magician. Invite a real magician to turn your party into a magical event.

For Ages: 6–9

Optional Ages: 2–5

Preparation: Find a professional magician by looking in the Yellow Pages under "Entertainers—Entertainment." You might also find magicians in the classified ads of your local newspaper or by calling magic shops for recommendations.

WHAT TO DO

You can find a magician through a special company or agency, or hire one that works independently. Interview several by phone ahead of time to determine which performance or act is right for your party and guests.

Your magician party can be fun and simple— just let the magician do all of the entertaining, and then have cake and ice cream afterwards. Videotape the performance if possible, and let the kids watch it once the magician leaves, for an added treat.

Before the magician arrives, pass out capes, hats, and wands and let the kids pretend to be magicians. Magic shops have lots of fun tricks, jokes, toys, cards, and books about magic that will keep the kids busy until the special entertainer arrives. (Or check out a magic book from the library and have some fun tricks ready to show the kids.) Take lots of photos before and during the show.

CREATIVE OPTIONS

• Instead of having tricks to hand out to the kids when they arrive at the party, ask the kids to prepare two or three tricks ahead of time to present when they arrive.

• Serve a "magic" dessert such as Jell–O with surprise fruit or candy inside, or pieces of cake with a surprise toy inside (warn them ahead of time!).

• Include a little magic trick inside the invitations to get the kids in the mood for a magical event.

For Added Fun:
- Magician's clothing (top hats and black capes) for all of the guests (available at magic shops and toy stores)
- Magic wands (available at magic shops and toy stores)

- Invite the guests with invitations written in invisible ink (available at toy stores) or milk that has dried on the paper (use a cotton swab for writing the party details). Give the guests instructions for reading the invitations (for the dried milk option, the paper must be heated until the letters appear).

PRIZES AND FAVORS

- Send the little magicians home with their new magic tricks.

- Let them keep the top hats, capes, and wands.

- Give everyone a Polaroid snapshot of themselves posing with the magician.

TROUBLE-SHOOTING TIP

- Remind the guests to be good listeners during the magic act and not to shout out solutions to the tricks.

CALL THE POLICE!

Kids see crime shows on TV all the time—invite a police officer to the party so the kids can find out what it's *really* like to be a cop. For an extra-special activity, have the kids solve a mysterious crime complete with clues, evidence, and a clever solution.

For Ages: 6–9

Optional Ages: 2–5, 10–12 for guest speaker; 10–12 for mystery

Preparation: Call a local police department to see if a police officer can come to the party in uniform with some equipment.

WHAT TO DO

When you call the police station, find out what items the police officer can bring for the presentation (such as "Wanted" signs, handouts, or posters). Be sure to determine the amount of time the police officer will be able to spend at the party—if it's a short time, have other activities planned.

As the guests arrive, give them police badges and hats to wear. Encourage them to ask the police officer questions if they want. When the special presentation is over, gather the kids for a "mystery activity" (you'll need to secretly set up a crime scene beforehand).

To create a crime scene (such as the mysterious disappearance of the cake), hide the cake and leave a note that says: "I have stolen the cake, and you'll never find it! Ha! Ha! Ha!—The

Shadow." Then secretly take one of the kids aside to be the culprit and set up some clues—leave some flour spilled on the kitchen counter and floor, and have the culprit leave some fingerprints and a footprint in the mess; then borrow a couple of hairs from the culprit to leave at the scene, as well as an accessory or article of clothing. Once the scene is complete, send the culprit back to the other room with instructions not to let on about the mystery.

Once the special guest leaves, tell the kids it's time for cake. When everyone is ready to eat, exclaim that the cake has been stolen and that the kids must solve the crime! Pass out some magnifying glasses and let them search for clues. If they're stumped, have the culprit confess. Once they have solved the crime, let them feast on the stolen property.

For Added Fun:
- Police hats and badges (available at toy stores)
- Plastic magnifying glasses
- Flour
- A piece of paper and a pencil or pen

CREATIVE OPTIONS

- Ask the police officer if it is possible to arrive in a squad car that the kids can explore, under supervision, during the party.

- Give the kids posterboard and felt-tip pens for creating "Wanted" posters.

- For the mystery, you can have the culprit take one of the gifts instead of the cake. Plant a piece of wrapping paper on the bottom of the thief's shoe (use tape to make it stick), or have the culprit leave a mysterious, inky thumbprint on the note.

PRIZES AND FAVORS

- Let the kids take their police hats, magnifying glasses, and badges home.

- Give the kids other police accessories, such as whistles, handcuffs, or doughnuts.

- Send everyone home with comic books that feature "super cops."

TROUBLE-SHOOTING TIPS

- Remind the kids to be good listeners when the guest arrives and reward those who listened quietly with a special sticker.

- If you find out ahead of time which items the officer will be bringing to the presentation, you can alert the kids so they won't be disappointed if they don't get to see real weapons.

KARATE KIDS

Kids love action movies that feature karate masters, so invite a martial arts expert to show off some moves and teach your crowd self-defense.

For Ages: 6–9

Optional Ages: 2–5, 10–12

Preparation: Find a professional martial arts instructor by looking in the Yellow Pages under "Karate." Ask whether a professional teacher or student can give the kids a brief introduction to the sport and do a demonstration of karate, judo, kung fu, or another martial art.

WHAT TO DO

When looking for an instructor, try to find one who is accustomed to teaching and working with kids. Interview several martial arts experts by phone ahead of time to determine which one is right for your party and guests. Some of these instructors will entertain your party guests at no charge because it's a form of free advertising for their business, but others might charge a fee. They might also recommend one of their top students if they're too busy to make the visit.

Arrange for the martial arts expert to do a demonstration for the kids, and to teach them a few simple moves. The entertainer will probably want to share a little bit of the history and philosophy of the martial arts, too. As soon as the guests arrive, provide them with karate-style clothing (some oversized white T-shirts tied at the waist with white strips cut from sheets). Have the kids put on the outfits and remove their shoes and socks to make it a little more authentic. Then let the kids watch the demonstration and try a few moves. If they're really lucky, the instructor might show them the trick of chopping a brick or board bare-handed (just be sure to warn the kids not to try the trick at home!).

CREATIVE OPTIONS

• Clear away the furniture and let the kids try the karate moves they learned. If the instructor has time to work with the kids individually, arrange for this, and keep the other kids busy with comic books featuring martial arts heroes.

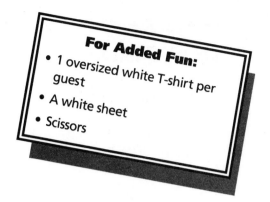

For Added Fun:
- 1 oversized white T-shirt per guest
- A white sheet
- Scissors

- Take Polaroid snapshots of each guest with the martial arts instructor. Tell the kids to pose in karate positions, for added fun.

- Rent the movie *The Karate Kid* and show it after the special guest leaves.

PRIZES AND FAVORS

- Give the kids books or comic books about the martial arts to take home.

- Let the kids wear their karate outfits home.

- Offer the kids Polaroid snapshots of themselves with the special entertainer.

TROUBLE-SHOOTING TIPS

- Remind the kids that the martial arts are a form of self-defense and should only be used as a defense against an attacker. (You don't want them to start roughhousing in the excitement!)

- Allow the kids lots of room to practice their kicks and karate chops so they won't hurt each other or themselves.

FUNNIEST HOME VIDEOS

Host a home version of the popular TV show, "America's Funniest Home Videos." Just invite a professional videotaper to create a great party video, and you'll have an event to remember!

For Ages: 6–9

Optional Ages: 10–12

Preparation: Find a professional video-taper by looking in the Yellow Pages under "Video." For a less-expensive alternative, rent or borrow a video camera and let a friend or family member do the job. If you don't have a VCR, you'll need to rent or borrow one.

WHAT TO DO

When trying to find a video expert, make sure the person you hire has a camera that's compatible with your VCR so you can play the tape during the party. Try to find a videotaper who can show the kids how the camera works and who is comfortable working with kids.

Before the special guest arrives, divide the kids into two groups and give them some time to come up with ideas for their own funny home video. (Or, for a smaller group, let all of the kids work together.) Put on some music and let the kids come up with a silly skit, commercial, or dance for the video. Provide costumes and old clothing to help them get inspired. Then let the videotaper record the first group of kids while you keep the other group entertained in a separate room, with comic books

or joke books. The videotaper can then film the second group. Later, bring everyone into the party room for a private screening complete with popcorn.

CREATIVE OPTIONS

• After the main event, ask the videotaper to go around the room and record each guest giving a special message or greeting to the guest of honor. This will provide priceless memories of the party!

• Have the kids bring their own home videos and show some clips to the crowd. Encourage the kids to choose something funny from their video collection and have them vote for the funniest home video of all.

• Move the guests one at a time into a separate room and have the videotaper get

For Added Fun:
- Costumes or old clothes (available at costume and thrift shops)
- Comic and joke books
- Popcorn
- Cassette tapes or records and a stereo

close-ups of body parts such as feet, fingers, or noses. Then have the guest talk in a funny voice. Repeat for all of the guests, then show the video to the crowd so they can try to guess who's who.

PRIZES AND FAVORS

- Send the kids home with inexpensive used videotapes from a video rental store.

- Give each guest a big bag of popcorn (store-bought or homemade) to eat while watching a favorite video at home.

- If you try the guessing game option, hand out prizes such as movie treats to anyone who shouts out a correct answer.

TROUBLE-SHOOTING TIPS

- Encourage the kids to be as silly as they want for the videos but not to get too rambunctious. Give special encouragement to any kids who seem shy in front of the camera.

- Take care of the videos brought from the kids' homes—they are very valuable to the owners.

ARTIST PARTY

Kids love making things with their hands. It's fun, enhances self-esteem, and creates a personalized, one-of-a-kind product. Invite an artist for a creative event!

For Ages: 6–9

Optional Ages: 2–5, 10–12

Preparation: Decide what type of artist you'd like to invite (try artists who specialize in ceramics, clay sculpture, painting, or collage). Contact an art store, college, or your child's teacher for artist referrals.

WHAT TO DO

When looking for an artist, try to find one who is accustomed to teaching and working with kids. Request that the artist bring samples of his or her work, and be sure you know ahead of time what type of art materials you'll need to have on hand for the kids to use (the artist might provide supplies, too). Specify on the invitations that the kids wear clothes that can get a little messy or that they bring smocks or old shirts.

Set up some tables in the party room (or the garage, if you're worried about a mess) and put newspapers over them. Then just let the artist take it from there. While the kids are busy doing their projects, make up some ribbons—one for each guest—that give a special award or honor for each project. (Make the ribbons out of construction paper and felt-tip pens.) Don't turn the activity into a contest—instead find something good about each piece of artwork.

CREATIVE OPTIONS

- Ask the kids to wear oversized white shirts to the party. Buy fabric paints (available at art supply stores) and let the kids paint their shirts after the artist leaves.

- Have the kids make their own stationery. Just buy rubber stamps and ink pads (available at toy stores, art supply stores, and card shops) and paper by the pound (available at card shops and party supply stores). Let the kids go wild!

- Purchase yards of shelf paper and have the kids make a mural! They can do body

For Added Fun:
- Construction paper
- Felt-tip pens
- Tables
- Newspapers
- Any art supplies needed for working with the artist

tracings and color all of the self-portraits—it makes a great gift for the guest of honor.

PRIZES AND FAVORS

- Send all of the kids home with their artwork and ribbons.

- Give everyone a supply of art materials—felt-tip pens, colored paper, or a box of paints and paintbrushes.

- Give the guests craft how-to books or posters by famous children's illustrators.

TROUBLE-SHOOTING TIPS

- Ask adult volunteers to help if the type of work the artist does is complicated. This will prevent the kids from getting confused or frustrated waiting for help.

- If the kids worry about not being good at art, tell them it's not a contest and that the goal is just to have fun.

- Give the guests special cleanup tasks after the activity (*e.g.*, washing paintbrushes or putting supplies away). This will make cleaning up easier for everyone, especially the guest artist.

Preteen 10-12

CHARADES

Kids love charades as much as adults do—it's a classic party-pleaser. Older kids might find the creative options even more fun and challenging.

For Ages: 10–12

Optional Ages: 6–9

Players Needed: 6 or more

Object: To guess the phrase or sentence your team is acting out, in the shortest period of time

HOW TO PLAY

Before the party, write some simple phrases, sentences, or book, movie, or song titles (appropriate for your party crowd) on slips of paper. Fold the papers up and place them in a hat, bowl, or other container.

At game time, divide the guests into two teams and seat them across from one another. Show the various pantomime signs used in Charades: open hands signify a book title; a cranking motion (for a pretend camera) signifies a movie title; and waving a hand before an open mouth signifies a song title; cupping a hand behind an ear means "sounds like"; holding up one finger means "first word" of the saying (two fingers, second word, and so on); and one finger inside the elbow means "first syllable"; a beckoning motion tells the audience they're close to the right answer; a pushing away motion tells them they're off base; and touching the nose indicates a correct response.

Have someone from the first team pick out a slip of paper and silently read the title or phrase. Give her one to three minutes, depending on the group's ability, to stand up before the group and communicate the information to her teammates without speaking. (The other team may watch the action, too.) Then let a player from the second team choose a slip of paper and communicate the information to her team, while everyone watches. Continue to trade off turns in this manner. Record the time it takes each team to get the right answers—the team with the least total amount of time wins the game (after everyone has had a chance to play performer).

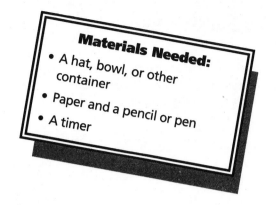

Materials Needed:
- A hat, bowl, or other container
- Paper and a pencil or pen
- A timer

CREATIVE OPTIONS

- Play a specific form of Charades, such as "Rock Music Charades" or "Scary Movie Charades," using any phrases, titles, or sentences from those categories.

- Play "One-Word Charades" with the players acting out a single word, such as "flat," "headache," "corner," and so on. (If you have trouble thinking up words, look at some of the one-word clues in the board game "Pictionary.")

- Play "People Charades" and have the players act out famous people instead of phrases and titles (include cartoon characters, politicians, movie stars, child actors, and historical figures).

- Allow the kids to write up the titles and phrases themselves, so they can have a shot at stumping the group.

PRIZES AND FAVORS

- Give the winning team small plastic "Oscar" awards (available at party supply stores).

- Hand out cassette singles of songs used in the game, or give away the board game version of Charades.

- Buy or make a large bag of popcorn for each guest to take home.

TROUBLE-SHOOTING TIPS

- Make a chart before the game showing the various Charades signals so there won't be any confusion.

- If a player is shy about performing for the others, just let her help with the guessing.

- If the teams write their own titles and phrases, screen them to weed out any that are too difficult.

149

GOSSIP

This party favorite always produces lots of laughs. You'll get the best results when you play it with a large group.

For Ages: 10–12

Optional Ages: 6–9

Players Needed: 8 or more

Object: To whisper a piece of gossip down the line of players and see how well the message was carried

HOW TO PLAY

Before the game, write out ridiculous bits of gossip about each of the guests on slips of paper—the more ludicrous the better. For example: "Yesterday, Nicole quit school, eloped with Luke Perry, and is planning to have eight children"; "Tom spent a year in jail when he was nine for stealing Snickers bars from the Snack Shack"; or "Rebecca got muscle implants, hair extenders, and a nose ring so she could look really cool."

At game time, arrange the players in a line or circle and show the first player one of the slips of paper. After he stops laughing, he must whisper the rumor to the next player, who whispers it to the next player, and so on down the line until the last player has heard the story. Have the last player recite the piece of

gossip *exactly* as he heard it—see how close to the truth he gets! Send the first player to the end of the line after the round and play again.

CREATIVE OPTIONS

• Let the kids make up their own outrageous rumors to be passed down the line (make sure to write them down so the comparison can be made).

• Cut out phrases from the tabloids, glue them to pieces of paper (substituting the names of the guests for the famous names), and use them for the gossip starters. The kids will get a kick out of hearing that "Heather is pregnant with the fifty-pound baby of an alien" or "Joey's botched facelift makes him look like Willard Scott."

Materials Needed:
- Enough space for the players to form a long line or large circle
- Paper and a pencil or pen

• Make the gossip appropriate to your party theme. If it's a dance party, write down rumors about rock groups or add the guests' names to song titles or lyrics. Or just make the pieces of gossip into tongue twisters so the message is sure to get mixed up.

PRIZES AND FAVORS

• Send everyone home with the piece of gossip about them taped to a goody bag or made to look like an award certificate.

• Give the kids the funny tabloid headlines with their names on them.

• Offer the guests teen magazines full of gossip (and remind them that everything they hear and read may not be true).

TROUBLE-SHOOTING TIPS

• When writing the rumors, don't make the sentences too long (the kids might get confused) or too short (the kids might find the game unchallenging).

• Don't write any rumors that could be true or embarrassing for the players—keep them completely silly.

• Remind the kids to whisper softly so only the receiver will hear the message. Play music in the background to obscure the messages.

SCAVENGER HUNT

What do an old shoelace, a paper clip, and a rock have in common? They're great items for a scavenger hunt. Searching for unusual items is the challenge, so when making your list, be creative—and a little crazy!

For Ages: 10–12

Optional Ages: 6–9

Players Needed: 3 or more

Object: To locate all the items (or as many as possible) on the list

HOW TO PLAY

Prepare a list of items for the kids to locate and photocopy it for each guest, or for each team, depending on how big the group is. You can play this game indoors or outdoors—just make sure your list reflects your choice. Try these suggestions or use your own: an old shoelace, a paper clip, lipstick, a tea bag, a party item, a rock, a bobby pin, an old paperback, a used eraser, some litter, a flower, unopened junk mail, a business card, dog food, a colored pencil, a receipt, a candy bar, and/or some sand.

At game time, define the area where the players can search and set a time limit; then divide the players into pairs, teams, or let them play solo. Pass out lists and bags and let them get started. When the players return,

dump out each bag and review the items to see if they brought back exactly what was on the list. The player or team with the most "acceptable" items wins.

CREATIVE OPTIONS

• Let each player make her own list, then pass it to another player who must find the items (teams can make up and exchange lists, too). Advise the kids not to make the items too easy or too hard, and review the lists to weed out impossible-to-find items.

• Offer bonus opportunities by making lists of generic items (for example, a shoelace) and adding beside them optional bonus items (a *colorful* shoelace). The kids can double their findings!

• Have a "white elephant scavenger hunt" where the teams go door-to-door asking for

Materials Needed:

- A timer
- 1 large bag per player or per team
- A photocopied list of items for each player or team to find (see suggestions in How to Play)
- Paper and a pencil or pen

a donation of anything strange, bizarre, and unwanted. (This option works best when you know the neighbors well.) Have the kids return to the party and see who collected the strangest stuff.

PRIZES AND FAVORS

- Give the winners a fun item from the scavenger hunt list.

- Give the losers a funny item from the list as a consolation prize.

- Send everyone home with goody bags full of small things like mini candy bars, Hershey's Kisses, small rubber balls, fun buttons, or sugarless bubblegum.

TROUBLE-SHOOTING TIPS

- Find adult volunteers to go along with the kids if you're having an outdoor hunt.

- Make some rules—"Be careful crossing streets," or "No searching in drawers and other private areas," etc. Set any other limits you think might be necessary.

- Don't make the scavenger items too difficult—the kids have more fun when they can find most of them.

ROMANCING THE STORY

Here's a game that doesn't have competition, but does create lots of laughs! All it takes is some imagination and creativity.

For Ages: 10–12

Optional Ages: 6–9

Players Needed: 5 or more

Object: To have the group create a humorous story

HOW TO PLAY

Give paper and pencils to all of the guests and have them sit in a circle. Let them know they are going to write a "best-selling romance story," section by section, working as a team.

Each player writes part of the story, following your instructions. Start the story with the girl character's name—have each player write her name and a description of her, then fold the paper over, and pass it to the next player. Next, have the writers come up with a boy's name and description, then fold the paper over, and pass it again. The kids should continue writing and passing the paper, using the following plot turns: how the boy and girl met, the first words the boy said to the girl, how the girl replied to the boy, what happened next, what the neighbors said, the

consequences, what the newspapers printed about them, and their future. When everyone has finished with the last paragraph, let them unfold the papers and read the funny stories aloud, one by one.

CREATIVE OPTIONS

• Distribute different-colored paper and pens to make the game even more fun.

• Get more creative with the plot lines, having animals or famous people as the characters. Or have the kids write a murder mystery or spy story.

• Host a "writer" party, with the guests starring as authors (you could provide fun props for them such as sunglasses or oversized pens or pencils to get them in the mood). Serve a cake shaped like an open book.

Materials Needed:
- Enough space for the players to form a circle
- Paper and a pencil or pen for each player

PRIZES AND FAVORS

- Give everyone popular preteen, joke, or cartoon books.

- Offer the kids journals and fancy pens so they can practice their writing at home.

- If you have a "writer" party, let the kids wear the props home.

TROUBLE-SHOOTING TIPS

- Divide each piece of paper into ten sections so the writers know exactly how much they can write and where the words should go.

- Set a time limit so the players will write quickly and spontaneously. If they get stuck, give them a few creative ideas.

SPOONS

The kids will soon find that half the fun of playing this exciting game is trying to quickly grab a spoon—and the other half is discovering they're the last to get one! This game is full of fast-paced fun.

For Ages: 10–12

Optional Ages: 6–9

Players Needed: 6 or more

Object: To secretly steal a spoon before anyone else

HOW TO PLAY

The players sit in a circle on the floor or at a table, with some spoons placed in the circle's center in a star-burst design (for easy access). There should be one less spoon in the middle of the circle than the number of players. Deal four cards to each player, put the remaining cards in a draw pile, and choose a leader (or play the leader yourself). The kids must collect four matching cards to pick up a spoon.

To play, the leader first chooses the top card from the draw pile and decides if she wants to keep it. Whether or not she keeps it, she must discard one card to the player on her right. That player, who is also trying to collect four matching cards, can keep or discard that card or another from her own hand. Play continues in this manner, with the players continually

passing cards to their right. Here's where it gets tricky: the player to the *left* of the leader doesn't discard to the leader but to a discard pile. (What usually happens is that the leader runs out of cards from the draw pile before anyone gets a set of four—she then begins pulling from the discard pile, and the player to her left starts a new discard pile). This game should move fast, and players should never have more than four cards at once. To keep the game going at a steady pace, shout: "Pass!" every so often to make the kids pass the cards quickly. The first player to get four matching cards must quickly and quietly grab a spoon from the middle of the circle. All of the other players must then grab one, too.

Usually the players get so carried away with collecting cards that they forget to watch the spoons and/or the other players. When all of

Materials Needed:
• A spoon for all but one player
• A deck of cards

the spoons are gone, and the last player is left with nothing but a look of surprise, begin another round with the loser starting the deal.

CREATIVE OPTIONS

• You don't have to play with spoons—any item that's easy to see and grab will work.

• Have the kids do a funny action rather than grabbing spoons or other items. For example, they can stick out their tongues or touch their noses once they've collected four matching cards.

• Have the player who didn't get a spoon stand up and do something silly, such as bark like a dog, or spin around like a ballerina.

PRIZES AND FAVORS

• Give the kids fun food items that must be

eaten with a spoon—pudding, Jell–O, or ice cream, for example—along with decorative or plastic spoons.

• Give everyone a deck of cards.

TROUBLE-SHOOTING TIPS

• Remember to use items that can withstand getting grabbed and squeezed by energetic hands (candy bars, for example, may get mushy if the kids aren't careful). Avoid paper items—they're apt to get mangled and torn.

• Be sure to enforce the "Pass" rule as much as possible. Otherwise, it's not fair for the kids sitting to the right of slow passers.

QUICK DRAW

This fast-paced drawing game has been a favorite for years. It doesn't require any artistic talent—the worse the kids draw, the more fun they'll have during the game.

For Ages: 10–12

Optional Ages: 6–9

Players Needed: 4 or more

Object: To guess the phrase, object, title, or sentence your teammate is drawing before the time is up

HOW TO PLAY

Before the party, write some simple objects, phrases, or sentences (appropriate for your party crowd) on slips of paper. Fold the papers up and place them in a hat, bowl, or other container. Try single words such as "spring," "hamburger," "basement," or "bride"; common phrases such as "Raining cats and dogs," "Quiet as a mouse," or "Not guilty"; or movie, TV, or song titles.

At game time, gather the guests around a table and divide them into two teams. A player on the first team must choose a card without looking and draw a picture that represents the word or phrase. (He must *draw* only—talking or gesturing is not allowed.) Set the timer for one, two, or three minutes, depending on the skill level of the kids. The player's teammates must try to guess what the word or phrase is before the time runs out. Give each team a point for a correct answer, and award a prize to the team with the most points at the end of the game. Or play a non-competitive version without points—just let the next team choose a new slip of paper and move on.

CREATIVE OPTIONS

- Let the teams make up their own words and phrases for the other teams to guess—screen them to weed out any that are too difficult.

- If a team is unable to guess what their player is drawing and the time runs out, pass the drawing to the other team to see if they can guess correctly.

Materials Needed:
- A table
- Large sheets of paper
- Felt-tip pens or pencils
- A hat, bowl, or other container
- A timer

- Play the game based on a specific category or theme, such as music, movies, or book titles.

- For a really silly game, have the kids draw with the hand they don't usually use, or with their eyes closed.

PRIZES AND FAVORS

- Give each player a pad of paper and a fun pencil so they can play the game at home.

- Send everyone home with drawing supplies—sketch pads, charcoal, or colored pencils (available at art supply stores).

- Offer the kids packs of felt-tip pens.

TROUBLE-SHOOTING TIPS

- Make sure the players have enough time to draw, but not too much time or the game won't be challenging.

- Switch team members around if one team continually wins.

RELAY RACES

Preteens love doing relays—the sillier, the better! They'll enjoy the exercise and the craziness of these zany games.

For Ages: 10–12

Optional Ages: 6–9

Players Needed: 6 or more

Object: To be the first team to reach the finish line after completing the required challenges

HOW TO PLAY

Get ready for your day of relays by preparing all of the materials ahead of time—first gather sacks, spoons, clothing, and oranges, and then hard-boil some eggs. Lay ropes on the grass (twenty-five feet apart is a good minimum distance) or, if you play indoors, clear away the furniture and mark starting and finishing lines with masking tape.

Start off with the Sack Relay. Divide the kids into two teams and have them line up behind the starting line. Have the first player on each team stand in a sack or pillowcase. The first players must hop to the finish line in the sacks, step out of them at the finish line, run back to the starting line with their sacks, and pass them to the next players in line. The race continues in this manner until every player on one team has completed the challenge.

Next, move on to some even sillier relays. For the Egg on the Spoon Relay, divide the kids into two teams and give each player a spoon. Give the first player on each team an egg (don't tell the kids the eggs are hard-boiled), and have them walk as quickly as possible to the finish line and back to the starting line, balancing the eggs on the spoons. Once the players reach the starting line again, they must carefully pass the eggs to the next players in line without touching the eggs! The race continues in this manner until every player on one team has completed the task. (If a player drops an egg, she must get a new egg and start again.)

The Orange Relay is sure to make the kids laugh, too. To play, divide the kids into two teams and have them form two lines; then have them pass an orange from the beginning of each line to the end, using only

Materials Needed:
- 2 burlap sacks or 2 large pillowcases
- A spoon for each player
- Hard-boiled eggs (the relay requires 2, but some might break)
- 2 oranges
- Ropes or masking tape to mark the starting and finishing lines

their chins and necks! If a player drops the orange at any time, she must pick it up without using her hands and continue.

CREATIVE OPTIONS

- Invite the guests' parents to join in the relays! The kids will love watching their parents compete in the races, and the games are great fun for adults, too.

- In the Orange relay, have the kids line up alternating male and female, if you wish. This game can serve as a good icebreaker.

PRIZES AND FAVORS

- Award small plastic trophies to everyone (available at party supply stores).

- Give the grand prize winner a book about a popular athlete.

TROUBLE-SHOOTING TIPS

- Play the games on a grassy surface and clear away any lawn debris. Or clear a large indoor area and remove any obstacles.

- If one team consistently wins, switch the players around after each race to make the competition more challenging.

- Don't put too much focus on competition.

TRUTH OR CONSEQUENCES

Here's a kids' game that's so fun even adults like it! It gives the guests a chance to take a dare and act really silly.

For Ages: 10–12

Optional Ages: 6–9

Players Needed: 6 or more

Object: To tell the truth or take the consequences

HOW TO PLAY

Before the game, write up some silly questions on slips of paper—some that are *slightly* embarrassing, and some that are easy. For example, you might ask: "Who is your girl-friend (boyfriend)?" or "What's the worst thing you ever did?"; or ask: "Is the sky blue?" or "How much is two plus one?" Fold up the slips of paper and place them in a small box, with the word "Truth" written on the outside.

Next, write up a set of stunts and tricks and place them in a separate box labeled "Consequences." Make up tricks that are silly and fun, such as "Sing the chorus of a popular rock song," "Call your mom and apologize for the last bad thing you did," or "Hop around the room like a kangaroo."

Gather the guests in a cozy circle and have the first player pick a slip of paper from the "Truth" box. He must read the question aloud to the group and make a choice—to answer the question truthfully or to lie. If he doesn't tell the truth, he must pick a consequence from the other box and perform the stunt. Once he has told the truth or taken a consequence, move on to the next player.

CREATIVE OPTIONS

• Write up consequences that take two players to perform, and then have a player choose another player to take the consequences with him. For example, have the two players race across the room on one foot, buzz like bees (seeing who can buzz the longest without taking a breath), or sing out loud.

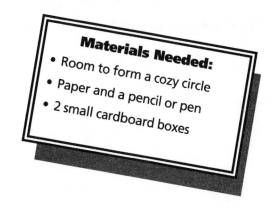

• Instead of asking personal questions or ones that are really easy, ask trivia questions about sports, U.S. capitols, or music. When a player can't answer a question correctly, have him do a funny stunt.

• Allow the guests to make up their own questions and stunts for each other. Screen them before the game to weed out any that are too difficult or embarrassing.

PRIZES AND FAVORS

• Send the kids home with boxes filled with small goodies.

• Give everyone a diary for keeping their secrets or lockets for storing personal photos.

• Take Polaroid snapshots of the kids doing silly stunts and pass them out at the end of the game.

TROUBLE-SHOOTING TIPS

• If the kids take too long deciding whether to answer the questions truthfully, use a timer.

• Some kids might need a little encouragement to do the tricks or stunts. Try modifying the "consequences" a little if it makes the kids feel more comfortable.

• Make the questions fun and silly, rather than too personal; make the consequences entertaining, rather than embarrassing.

CHAOS CARDS

This fast-paced, action-packed card game is great for a group of quick thinkers—just when they think they've got it down, it's chaos!

For Ages: 10–12

Optional Ages: 6–9

Players Needed: 4 or more

Object: To have the most cards when the time is called

HOW TO PLAY

Have the players sit in a circle (on the floor or at a table) and deal all of the cards face down. If you have more than four players, use two decks of cards, and if there are more than eight players, use three decks. Tell the kids not to look at their cards. On the posterboard, draw symbols of the four suits: a heart, a diamond, a club, and a spade, as well as a symbol for numbers—"#." Ask the players to name a category, such as "girls' names," and write that category next to the first symbol. Next, ask for another category, such as "boys' names," and write it beside the next symbol. Repeat this three more times, until each symbol has a different category next to it. (Some fun categories are candy bars, cars, singers, or foods.) Have the players memorize the categories, but keep the chart visible.

Whenever you say, "Chaos!" all of the players must flip over one card *at the same time,* then scan the overturned cards to see if their card matches the suit or number of any other cards. The players who match suits must shout out an item in the category that corresponds with the suit. For example, if two players flip cards showing hearts, they must race to name an item in the "girls' names" category; if three players flip cards showing clubs, they must race to name an item in whatever category has been assigned to clubs. Here's the catch: any cards with matching *numbers* take precedence over cards with matching suits. So, if two players flip matching fives, and two others flip matching diamonds, the kids with matching fives are the ones to race to name an item from the "#" category. As you can see, this game is chaos! The player who correctly yells out a category item first wins all

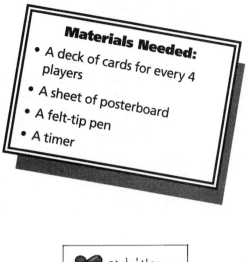

Materials Needed:
- A deck of cards for every 4 players
- A sheet of posterboard
- A felt-tip pen
- A timer

of the cards that were turned face up during the round. Set a timer for twenty minutes and see who has the most cards at that time—keep playing if the kids love the game.

CREATIVE OPTIONS

- For a simpler game, assign categories for suits only. In other words, only cards that match suits count.

- Tell the players that words used to win a round cannot be repeated. For example, if a player calls out the name "Mary" before any other players to win the round, that name can't be called when the girls' names category comes up again.

- After the kids have played using the first set of categories, stop the game and write in new ones on the back of the posterboard.

The kids will have to learn a new set of categories and forget the old set—more chaos!

PRIZES AND FAVORS

- Give everyone their own deck of cards to take home.

- Send them home with some items from the categories, such as candy bars, small toys, or snacks.

- Offer the game winner a fancy deck of cards.

TROUBLE-SHOOTING TIPS

- Don't wait too long to shout "Chaos!" or the kids will have time to prepare their answers, rather than thinking them up spontaneously.

- Jot down any category items used, so that repeat items can be disqualified.

PUZZLE BAGS

If you have a big group of guests who don't know each other very well, this is the perfect game for you. It's a quiet icebreaker that will help your group get ready for more games and activities.

For Ages: 10–12

Optional Ages: 6–9

Players Needed: 6 or more

Object: To be the first team to figure out their puzzle bag's theme

HOW TO PLAY

Prepare some "puzzle bags" by deciding on a fun theme for each bag and gathering the appropriate items. Here are some suggestions: School (ruler, pencil, dunce cap, apple, lunch bag, late slip); Pizza (olives, flour, water, cookbook, cheese, Italian spices); Monopoly (an iron, a shoe, a hotel receipt, dice, money); "Beverly Hills 90210" (sunglasses, money, a postcard from Minnesota, a zip code, a picture of sideburns); or the Beach (sand, water, tanning oil, a bikini top, a lifeguard whistle, "Shark Bites" candy). Just make sure the themes relate to preteens and that the items aren't too abstract.

At game time, divide the guests into teams and give each team a bag of items. They must take the items out of the bags, look them over, and decide what they have in common. The first group to figure out the theme of their bag wins.

CREATIVE OPTIONS

- Have the teams write down their answers instead of calling them aloud. When the teams have written down their answers, they can hand them to you, exchange bags, and play again.

- Play the game using words written on slips of paper, rather than using actual items.

- Play as one large group, holding up one item at a time from the bags and allowing everyone to guess the theme.

- If the party has a special theme, design the "puzzle bags" with that theme in mind. For

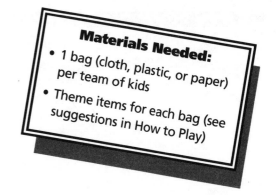

Materials Needed:
- 1 bag (cloth, plastic, or paper) per team of kids
- Theme items for each bag (see suggestions in How to Play)

example, if it's a dance party, fill each of the bags with items related to different musical groups or song lyrics.

PRIZES AND FAVORS

- Buy colorful bags from a party supply store, fill them with goodies, and let the kids on the winning team take them home after the party (or give one to each child).

- Fill a bag with snacks for a "Junk Food" theme, and distribute the goodies after the game. Or let the kids reach in the bag without looking and pick their "prize."

- Give the kids some of the items from the bags—but only the fun stuff.

TROUBLE-SHOOTING TIP

- Try to put together "puzzle bags" with the same degree of difficulty. It isn't fair to the other teams if one team's bag is really simple.

" SCHOOL"

167

MYSTERY MELODIES

Much like the old TV game show "Name That Tune," this musical game is fast, frenzied, and lots of fun.

For Ages: 10–12

Optional Ages: 6–9

Players Needed: 3 or more

Object: To be the first to correctly name the most tunes

HOW TO PLAY

Prerecord lots of sample lyrics from your preteen's music collection or record bits of various songs from her favorite radio station. (Make sure to write down the song titles and musical artists, if you're not familiar with them.) Record about thirty seconds of silence between the songs, too.

To start the game, have the guests sit in a circle and play only the first set of notes for the first song. The first player to call out the name of the song wins a point (she can earn a bonus point for correctly naming the singer or group). If none of the players can get the answer, play a little bit more of the song. If that doesn't help, move on. Continue in this manner until the whole tape is played. Make sure to record each player's points to see who got the most at the end of the game.

CREATIVE OPTIONS

- When recording songs for the tape, throw in a few oldies, some country music selections, or some famous tunes from musicals. Award extra points to players who guess the titles correctly.

- In addition to naming the song title and artist, have the guests identify the year the song came out or another bit of trivia.

- Have a rock-and-roll party with a dance or lip-sync contest. For added fun, hang musical decorations in the party room and ask the guests to dress as favorite pop stars.

PRIZES AND FAVORS

- Give the game winner a gift certificate to a record store or an inexpensive music video.

Materials Needed:
- Cassette player
- A blank cassette tape
- A selection of various recorded songs and artists
- Paper and a pencil or pen

- Send the gang home with blank cassette tapes, or buttons and/or postcards with popular performers on them.

- Give each guest a rock star poster or popular cassette single.

TROUBLE-SHOOTING TIPS

- If it's too chaotic when everyone calls out the song title at once, let the players guess one at a time. Just make sure each player has a turn to be the first guesser.

- Be sure to record enough of each song so that the players will eventually be able to get the right answer.

CRAZY OLYMPICS

Here is a great idea for an outdoor preteen party—host a Crazy Olympics with lots of fun challenges. The kids will love the physical exercise!

For Ages: 10–12

Optional Ages: 6–9

Players Needed: 6 or more

Object: To be the first to complete the challenges in each event

HOW TO PLAY

Divide the kids into teams of two, and start the Olympic games with a crazy obstacle course. Have two players compete at the same time on two identical courses. You'll have to set up a series of starting and finishing lines all around the yard so the kids can go from one challenge to another without stopping. Also tie a string or rope around two trees or two clothesline poles for the limbo (the trees or poles should be about five feet apart, and the rope about four feet off the ground).

For the first obstacle, have the kids balance an apple on their head and walk to the finish line, without dropping it. If the apple falls, it's back to the starting line for that player. For the second challenge, have the kids run backwards on all fours (crab-walking)—it's crazy,

but it can be done. Next, make the kids do the limbo! Show them how to bend backward and walk under the rope without letting the rope touch their stomach. For the final event, have the kids get on tricycles and pedal to the finish line as quickly as possible. After the first two players have completed the course, the next two players can begin.

For the last event, have the kids play a game of Leapfrog. After the kids have completed the other challenges, divide them into two teams, and put ropes on the ground to mark the starting and finishing lines. To play, the first player on each team must squat down, with shoulders and head tucked. The other players on each team line up single file and, one by one, "leapfrog" over their teammate (to leapfrog, a player simply places his hands on the stooped-over player's back and vaults

Materials Needed:
- A large, grassy outdoor space
- 2 tricycles
- 2 apples
- Ropes to mark the starting and finishing lines, plus an extra rope for the limbo
- 2 trees or 2 poles for the limbo

over him, legs apart). After the first players have completed the leapfrog, they must bend into a stooped position a few feet in front of the players they leaped over, and the next players must leapfrog over *two* players. Play continues like this until one team leapfrogs all of its players over the finish line.

CREATIVE OPTIONS

- Before the events begin, play a cassette tape of the Olympics theme music (or any music that is similar).

- Take lots of Polaroid snapshots of the kids performing during the events (the photos are fun for the kids to keep and compare during the party, and they serve as nice mementos). Then take one photo of the whole group of "Olympic Stars" and send reprints to everyone later, if you wish.

- If you can't set up two identical courses, have each player perform the feats separately. Use a timer to see who finishes first.

PRIZES AND FAVORS

- Give each guest a ribbon that says "First Place," "Second Place," "Honorable Mention," etc. You can find these at sports stores or make them yourself.

- Offer the grand prize winner a piece of sporting equipment.

TROUBLE-SHOOTING TIPS

- Demonstrate all of the challenges before the events begin so that the players understand what they must do.

- Play the games on a grassy surface and clear away any lawn debris.

- Don't put too much focus on competition.

BOX OFFICE TRIVIA

Kids love following the lives of celebrities and teen idols. Here's a fun trivia game that features questions about the stars. For extra fun, add a personal twist to the game by playing Friend Trivia, as well.

For Ages: 10–12

Optional Ages: 6–9

Players Needed: 4 or more

Object: To correctly answer the most trivia questions about celebrities or friends

HOW TO PLAY

Before the game, collect pictures and post-cards of various celebrities, and find some information about these stars, using magazines or books. You might use information like birthdates, hometowns, real names, girl-friends' or boyfriends' names, film/TV show titles, names of their film/TV characters, and some of their most famous lines. (Make sure you choose celebrities that preteens know well.) Write up the trivia questions on slips of paper, and place the postcards and pictures around the party room.

At game time, pass out the paper and pencils and tell the guests to answer each question secretly on paper. Ask the trivia questions, giving the guests some time to write down their answers. Plan on asking about twenty-five questions total. When all of the questions have been asked, let each guest reveal her answers. Award a prize to the guest who answered the most correctly. Then play a bonus round—this time with trivia questions about the various guests. (You'll have to come up with some questions ahead of time and secretly phone the guests' parents for the correct answers—try some about their favorite stuffed animals, which movie stars they have a crush on, what they did the last time they got in trouble, their favorite dessert, their favorite rock group, their best subject in school, etc.) Let the guests answer aloud in this version. See how well they know each other!

CREATIVE OPTIONS

• Write up some bonus questions that are a little more difficult, and award extra points

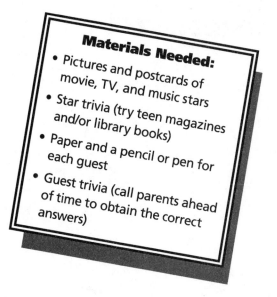

Materials Needed:
- Pictures and postcards of movie, TV, and music stars
- Star trivia (try teen magazines and/or library books)
- Paper and a pencil or pen for each guest
- Guest trivia (call parents ahead of time to obtain the correct answers)

for them. Try trivia about older movie stars or music groups to test the kids.

- Have the kids dress up as movie stars (you can provide sunglasses or other props). Serve star-shaped cookies and a star cake.

- Write up some trivia questions about the guest of honor and have the guests try to answer them. You can make them difficult or easy, but not too embarrassing!

PRIZES AND FAVORS

- Let each trivia game winner pick a celebrity picture or postcard to take home; or buy a special celebrity poster for the winner.

- Give all of the guests teen magazines, posters, or giant bags of popcorn.

- Award a small prize to any guest who answers a "friend trivia" question correctly (try cassette singles or celebrity buttons).

TROUBLE-SHOOTING TIPS

- If you plan to use dialogue from the movies for extra trivia questions, rent a few movies and jot down some of the best lines. Record several, so that if guests miss one, they can try again.

- When calling parents to find out trivia information about the guests, don't ask embarrassing or private questions.

- Ask an equal number of questions about each guest so no one feels left out. Tell each guest to remain silent when they're the subject of a question.

MURDERER

This game is scary, suspenseful, and full of surprises. Who will be the victim? And who will be the murderer? The answers are in a deck of cards.

For Ages: 10–12

Optional Ages: 6–9

Players Needed: 6 or more

Object: To solve the murder mystery before the other players

HOW TO PLAY

Write down a short and silly murder synopsis (small enough to fit on a playing card) on a slip of paper. Include the weapon, the motive, and the murder location. For example, you might write down the following: "The victim was killed with a squirt gun in an alley because she was blackmailing the murderer about the money stolen from the ice cream truck." Tape the slip of paper securely onto the face of the Ace of Spades. (Don't wrap the tape around the sides of the card.) Shuffle the cards and pass them out to all of the guests. Tell the players to look over their cards secretly to see if they have the Ace of Spades or the Joker. The player holding the Joker is the Victim, and the player with the Ace and information sheet is the Murderer. The Murderer must discreetly memorize the crime

information, and everyone must tuck their cards out of sight.

Flick the lights off and on for a moment. While the lights are out, the Victim must fall to the floor, pretending to be dead. When the lights are turned on again, have the rest of the players ask each other questions about the murder (including the Murderer, who remains anonymous). The Murderer must answer any questions truthfully, according to the information on the card. The other players should try to fool one another as they're asking and answering questions. The one question they can't ask, however, is: "Are you the Murderer?" The players can write down any information in their notebooks. The person who first discovers the culprit, weapon, motive, and murder location wins the game.

Materials Needed:
- A deck of cards with 1 Joker
- Tape
- A pencil or pen for each player
- A small notebook for each player

CREATIVE OPTIONS

- Write up funny scenarios on all of the cards. For example, you might write: "You're the maid. You were out of town during the murder. Your hand is too shaky to handle a weapon." The players can use these alibis as answers during questioning to make the game more intriguing.

- Write some instructions on the Joker card to add a little humor, such as "Roll over and play dead."

PRIZES AND FAVORS

- Give the "detectives" a sleuth kit, with a plastic magnifying glass and a "Holmes" hat.

- Offer the kids mystery novels (like Nancy Drew or the Hardy Boys mysteries), or solve-it-yourself mystery books.

- Give the kids mystery movie videos or the board game "Clue."

TROUBLE-SHOOTING TIPS

- If the kids have trouble knowing what type of questions to ask each other, offer suggestions and ask a few questions yourself. Or write up some sample questions on cards and pass them out.

- If the "sleuths" are completely stumped, ask each player to offer a clue to the group—all but one will be false.

"SNIFF SNIFF"

JINGLES AND SLOGANS

Preteen kids generally know the words to as many commercials as pop songs. Here's a fun way for them to use that knowledge.

For Ages: 10–12

Optional Ages: 6–9

Players Needed: 4 or more

Object: To correctly name the most products after hearing their jingles

HOW TO PLAY

Before the game, prerecord a collection of commercials (perhaps ten to fifteen total) from radio or TV. Leave a few seconds of silence between each jingle, and blank out the product's name in each song.

Gather the players together and distribute paper and pencils. Play the first jingle on a cassette tape, presenting a few notes of the music and lyrics (but not the product name). Have the players write down the name of the product the jingle is advertising. Once you've gone through all the jingles, read off the answers and see who got the most correct.

Next, play the "slogan" version of this game by writing down some old and new product slogans. For example, you might include "Catch the Wave!" (Coke), "I love what you do

for me!" (Toyota), and "It's Grrrreat!" (Frosted Flakes). Have the kids identify the product from the slogan.

CREATIVE OPTIONS

- Make a visual presentation by videotaping portions of TV commercials. Since seeing the commercials makes them easier to identify, record only a few seconds so the game will still be challenging.

- Instead of having the kids write their answers down on paper, have them call out their answers and race to see who can name the product first.

- Play the slogan version, letting the kids come up with their own slogan challenges.

- Instead of recording only a small amount of each jingle, record the entire jingle and play

Materials Needed:
- Blank cassette tape
- Cassette player
- Paper and pencils for each player

a little bit at a time. Have the players write down their answers as soon as they know the product, and record whether they got the correct answer on the first, second, or third play.

PRIZES AND FAVORS

- Give the kids one of the products mentioned in the jingles and slogans, such as a candy bar, a box of cereal, or a toy.

- Give everyone a gift certificate for a drugstore or toy store so they can pick out their favorite products.

- Let the grand prize winner take home the board game "Adverteasing."

TROUBLE-SHOOTING TIP

- Use commercials that kids are familiar with, and try to choose ones that feature products that preteens use. Avoid products for adults only, such as cigarettes and alcohol.

ROB YOUR NEIGHBOR

Here's a memory game that's fun for older kids since it has an element of suspense. It gives them a chance to win prizes that kids of all ages love—candy!

For Ages: 10–12

Optional Ages: 6–9

Players Needed: 6 or more

Object: To remember which player has stolen your favorite treat so you can get it back

HOW TO PLAY

Gather the kids in a circle on the floor and place a pile of candy bars in the center of the circle. Shuffling a deck of cards thoroughly, pass out three cards to each player and have the kids place the cards face up in front of them. Using a second deck (also shuffled), pick cards from the pile one at a time and hold them up for the kids to see. If a card matches one of the player's cards, he may take his favorite candy bar from the center pile. (Tell him to tuck the candy bar out of sight, so the other players can't see it, and tell the others to remember what he took). Continue in this manner until all of the candy bars are gone—each player should end up with three.

Next, reshuffle the first deck and give each player one card, telling the kids to peek at

them secretly. Return to the second deck of cards and display one card at a time—until one of the players has a match with his hidden card. After he proves it's a match, he can choose a candy bar to "steal" from another player, but he must first identify the candy bar and who originally took it. This isn't easy considering how many candy bars have been distributed! If he is able to name another player's hidden candy bar in one try, he may rob that player of it, leaving that player with only two candy bars. But if he incorrectly identifies the player who took a particular candy bar, he must give one of his own candy bars to that player. Play continues until everyone has had a chance to rob their neighbors.

CREATIVE OPTIONS

- Try small toys or other fun items, rather than candy bars, for the kids to "steal." Or play

Materials Needed:
• 3 mini candy bars for each player (different brands)
• 2 decks of cards

with wrapped hard candies, different brands of gum, trading cards, stickers, or buttons.

• Increase the number of candies or toys to make the game more difficult. (Reduce the number of candies for younger kids.)

• Instead of giving the kids only one guess when robbing their neighbors, give them two or three.

PRIZES AND FAVORS

• Let the kids keep their "loot"—make sure you have extras for any player who was left with no candy.

• Send the kids home with decks of cards.

• Make goody bags for the kids to store their candy, or buy goody bags at a party supply store.

TROUBLE-SHOOTING TIP

• If a player loses all of his candy and seems upset, tell him an insurance policy covered the loss. Then give him a giant candy bar for being a good sport.

EYEWITNESS

Preteens will love the drama and challenge of Eyewitness. The game can be played as many times as the kids like, always with a different outcome.

For Ages: 10–12

Optional Ages: 6–9

Players Needed: 4 or more

Object: To recall the most details of a crime

HOW TO PLAY

You'll have to do a little planning before the party to make sure this game is a success. First, find an adult volunteer who will act as the robber during the game, and put an appropriate costume together. Set the stage for the crime by creating a scene or display, using various props. For example, if the crime is a jewelry heist, set up display tables with costume jewelry, make price tags, and put up a jewelry store sign.

When the guests arrive, choose one to play the sales clerk, and give her a name tag made from construction paper that tells who she is. The rest of the kids can be customers at the jewelry store. Have them take their places in the scene and tell them to expect the unexpected! This is your volunteer's cue—he or she enters the scene dressed as a robber, causes a commotion, steals a piece of jewelry, and leaves the scene, all within a few seconds. After the crime has been committed, ask the guests a series of questions about the robbery such as: "What was the robber wearing?" "What time did the robber enter the scene?" "What piece of jewelry was taken?" and "What did the robber look like?" Have the kids call out their answers, and record them to see who got the most correct—award a prize to that "super sleuth." You can play again, with the robber stealing a different item and changing his or her appearance. The second time you play, the kids will know that something is going to happen. They'll be more observant, which is fine, because they'll solve the crime sooner.

Materials Needed:
- A burglar costume: a mask, dark clothing, a "loot" bag, etc. (available at thrift shops and toy stores)
- An object to be stolen: a toy, a piece of jewelry, or a goody bag
- Props for the scene of the crime (see How to Play, for ideas)
- Construction paper
- Felt-tip pens
- Paper and a pencil or pen

CREATIVE OPTIONS

- Use other scenarios, such as a "fist fight" between two people, a murder, a different type of robbery, or a rude party-crasher.

- Create other crime scenes by turning your party room into a dance hall, a bank, a cruise ship, or another fun scene.

- Allow the kids to interview the suspect so they can solve the crime (the robber can lie or tell the truth, depending on how difficult you want the game to be).

PRIZES AND FAVORS

- Give everyone a magnifying glass.

- Present the big winner with a mystery game, such as "Clue" or "Lie Detector."

- Send the kids home with mystery books or give them items related to the crime scene, such as jewelry for a jewelry heist.

TROUBLE-SHOOTING TIPS

- If the kids don't pay close attention and miss some of the details the first time around, have the robber repeat the crime.

- If the kids have trouble figuring the mystery out, ask more specific questions such as, "Was the robber wearing a baseball cap or a sailor's hat?"

181

BABY BOTTLE RACE

Once the party-goers get warmed up with a few challenging games, they'll be ready for some hilarious activities. The kids will love getting a chance to act silly!

For Ages: 10–12

Optional Ages: 6–9

Players Needed: 2 or more

Object: To empty the baby bottle first

HOW TO PLAY

Before the race, fill each baby bottle with about two inches of water. Divide the kids into pairs (or play relay-style if you have a really big group, with the first set of players going first and other sets of players starting when they're done—just make sure everyone gets their own bottle). Have them put on baby bibs, if you choose to use them. At the starting signal, each of the two players must empty their bottles—by drinking out of them like a baby! The first one to drink all of his water wins. Then have the next pair race.

Since the bottle race is short, you might want to have the kids do another silly activity as long as they're in a silly mood. One at a time, have each guest close his eyes and have another guest speak to him in baby talk. The

first player must guess who is speaking. Play until everyone has had a turn to guess and talk baby talk.

CREATIVE OPTIONS

• Fill the baby bottles with more water for a longer race.

• Use juice or another liquid, rather than water.

• Try an activity called "Only a Face a Mother Could Love." Give the guests some tape and have them tape up their faces in funny ways. Tell them this is the way they looked when they were first born. Take Polaroid snapshots of each guest with a funny face.

• Serve teething biscuits and Cheerios, drinks in baby bottles, and a cake with all of the

Materials Needed:
- 1 baby bottle per player (use new nipples, if possible, for a more challenging game)
- *Optional:* baby bibs

kids' names on it, decorated with pink and blue frosting.

PRIZES AND FAVORS

• Send everyone home with their baby bottles.

• Give the big babies boxes of animal crackers to take home.

• Give each race winner a small stuffed animal, baby rattle, or pacifier.

TROUBLE-SHOOTING TIP

• If you want to use another beverage for the bottle race, try juice or punch, rather than a bubbly drink.

PRODUCT-ABILITY

Here's another fun icebreaker to get the kids in a party mood. Play more than once if the kids really like it.

For Ages: 10–12

Optional Ages: 6–9

Players Needed: 6 or more

Object: To guess which product you've been assigned

HOW TO PLAY

Cut out a product advertisement for each guest at the party. Try to choose items that will appeal to the kids to make the game more fun. You might include advertisements for products like Snickers bars, Coke, and *Seventeen* magazine, or various toothpastes and cereals. Keep the product ads in a bag by the front door, and as each guest enters the party, tape or pin the product ad to her back. Tell the kids there's something "going on behind their backs," but they can't look over their shoulders, use a mirror, or bribe other guests to tell them what it is.

To guess the products they have on their backs, the guests must ask questions such as, "Can this product be eaten" or "Is the product something to wear?" They are not allowed to

ask any direct questions such as, "What product am I?" Players can also give each other clues. For example, for a player who has a picture of a Coke can on her back, someone could say, "Are you thirsty?" "Can I get you a soft drink?" or "What a classic you are." When each guest finally guesses her product, she collects a prize.

CREATIVE OPTIONS

• Instead of using magazine ads, use the actual product packages and wrappers. For example, use a Snickers wrapper, a cover from *Seventeen* magazine, or an empty toothpaste tube.

• Use products in the same category. If your category is candy bars, find wrappers or ads for all different brands. This will make it a little easier for the kids to guess.

Materials Needed:
- 1 product advertisement per guest, clipped from a magazine
- A bag
- Tape or pins

- Play a version of this game with the kids guessing their "new identity" rather than a product name. Just pin the name of a sports star or celebrity on each player's back and have the players ask questions or give clues accordingly.

PRIZES AND FAVORS

- Give each guest the actual product once they guess what it is. But if a player is "toothpaste," for instance, you might want to give her a small treat, too.

- Give the kids favors related to their products, such as giant candy bars to match the small wrappers on their backs.

- If you play the celebrity identity version, give each player an item featuring their celebrity, such as a poster, postcard, or button, etc.

TROUBLE-SHOOTING TIPS

- In case the kids have trouble coming up with clues for the products, have a few clues ready ahead of time to help the players.

- Make sure the products are fun and well-known to kids (try products related to food, music, make-up, sports, clothes, or school subjects). Avoid ads for adult products only, such as cigarettes or alcohol.

REWRITE

Here is a homemade version of the popular game "Madlibs." Kids love the wacky results of Rewrite!

For Ages: 10–12

Optional Ages: 6–9

Players Needed: Any group size

Object: To create a crazy story

WHAT TO DO

Clip out articles or stories from teen magazines or other sources (one for each player). Choose articles that will take approximately sixty seconds to read aloud. Using White-Out, remove a number of adjectives, adverbs, nouns, and verbs from each story; or, if you have a typewriter or computer, type up the stories with those parts of speech missing. Underneath each blank, write whether the missing word was a noun, verb, adjective, or adverb. (If the articles have small type and seem hard to read after you erase some of the words, take them to a copy store and have them slightly enlarged.)

At game time, divide the kids into pairs and give a different story to each team. Have one team member read aloud the missing parts of speech (*not* the rest of the story though) for the other team member to fill in. In other words, Player One says, "Noun," and Player Two chooses a random noun for Player One to write in. This continues until each blank is filled in. When all of the kids have finished their rewrites, have them take turns reading their funny stories aloud. The result will be some crazy stories and lots of laughter!

CREATIVE OPTIONS

• Rather than erasing only nouns, verbs, adjectives, and adverbs, blank-out some complete quotations, names, or other appropriate items for the kids to fill in.

• Have all of the teams use the same story; then let them read their different versions. The kids will enjoy seeing how different the stories turn out.

Materials Needed:
- Articles from teen magazines, newspapers, or tabloids
- Liquid correcting fluid (e.g., White-Out)
- A pencil for each player

- Gather the kids in a circle and read out the missing parts of speech yourself, letting the kids shout out their suggestions. Write in the first one that you hear. It's fun when the game is a group effort.

PRIZES AND FAVORS

- Let the kids keep the funny stories—make sure you have one for each child.

- Give each guest a "Madlibs" activity tablet to take home.

- Give everyone a popular teen magazine or funny tabloid newspaper.

TROUBLE-SHOOTING TIPS

- If the kids have trouble thinking up words, quickly write up a list of suggestions to get them going.

- Encourage the kids to think up silly words to fill in the blanks—for instance, words like "giant" or "pig" make funnier stories than words like "man" or "person."

- Before the game, review the different parts of speech to help avoid confusion.

FREAKY FRIDAY

This crazy activity is inspired by the classic Disney film, *Freaky Friday.* You'll have to do some careful planning before hosting this delightfully twisted party—but the results are memorable! Everyone will have fun when the preteen guests come dressed as their parents and vice versa.

For Ages: 10–12

Optional Ages: 6–9

Players Needed: A group of kids *and* parents

Object: To have the kids and their parents switch roles

WHAT TO DO

This party requires both the preteens and one of their parents to attend, so call ahead of time to make sure both can come. Ask them to arrive dressed as one another, and encourage them to exaggerate as they're dressing up, for added humor. Be sure to let the guests know that daughters can dress as their fathers and sons as their mothers—either parent can attend! Also, have all of the guests answer some trivia questions that you've prepared ahead of time such as, "What time does your daughter really go to sleep at night?" "What kind of after-shave does your dad wear?" or "What's your child's favorite rock group?" Make sure the parents and kids answer these questions secretly so the answers will be a surprise at the party.

When the guests arrive, tell them they must talk and act like one another for the duration of the party. The parents will enjoy using slang, and the kids will like telling their parents what to do for a change! Play a trivia game by asking the questions you prepared before the party. Go around the room, letting the guests answer the questions in turn. Award prizes for questions answered correctly.

CREATIVE OPTIONS

• Instead of giving the guests time to come up with a Freaky Friday outfit, invite them by phone, asking them to arrive as one another—as they appear at the moment of the call.

• Play a general trivia game about parents and kids. Prepare some questions ahead of time

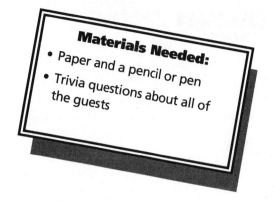

Materials Needed:
- Paper and a pencil or pen
- Trivia questions about all of the guests

that the parents must answer, and some that the kids must answer. For example, you might ask the parents, "Is Skid Row the name of a song, a rock group, or a jeans label?" You might ask the kids, "How much does gas cost per gallon?" Each group can confer before answering—award a point for each correct answer. The group with the most points at the end of the game wins.

PRIZES AND FAVORS

- Give the guests items appropriate to their new "identities" and let them trade when they get home (teen idol posters for the adults and cookbooks for the kids, etc.).

- Offer everyone joke gifts that stereotype parents and kids, such as teen magazines or copies of *Good Housekeeping.*

TROUBLE-SHOOTING TIPS

- If a parent is unavailable for the party, tell the child to bring a grandparent, relative, or adult friend.

- Encourage the guests to *really* exaggerate their imitations of one another—it helps them get into the spirit of their new roles.

TALENT SHOW

Kids love to show off, and what they lack in talent, they make up with enthusiasm. Give them a chance to put on a show for one another with a come-one, come-all talent show.

For Ages: 10–12

Optional Ages: 6–9

Players Needed: Any group size

Object: To put on a fun talent show

WHAT TO DO

When you invite the talented guests, don't tell them that you're planning a talent show. Half the fun is coming up with ideas on the spur of the moment. Arrange a stage by spreading sheets on the floor and tacking them to the wall for a background, and set up chairs for the audience.

Welcome the guests to the talent show by telling them they have just been hired by a famous producer to put on a show. Show them your collection of props, fashions, make-up, and music and tell them to get creative. They can work in teams or solo—just be sure to give them at least twenty minutes to prepare. Make suggestions to get them thinking about their talent: lip-sync to a pop song, sing a camp song, act out a skit, do a

popular dance, perform a parody of a TV show or musical, write and read a scary poem, show off some card tricks, or do a comedy routine. Then set up the video camera and start the show. When the show is over, play the video for more laughs.

CREATIVE OPTIONS

- Borrow some short plays from the library or rent video musicals that feature a number of roles for kids or teens (such as *Grease* or *Annie*). Then make up scripts, let the kids choose characters to act out, and let them put on a play or musical! Or rent a Karaoke machine so the kids can sing along.

- Videotape the performance and keep the camera rolling during the rehearsals, moving from room to room as the kids prepare for

Materials Needed:
- All sorts of fun clothing, costumes, props, and make-up
- A cassette player and musical tapes
- Chairs
- Sheets
- Thumbtacks
- *Optional:* a video camera and VCR

the show. You'll capture a behind-the-scenes look at the world of "show business."

- If you don't have a video camera, take Polaroid snapshots of the kids in costume, putting on their performances.

PRIZES AND FAVORS

- Give each performer a bouquet of flowers or a single rose when they come off the stage.

- Give everyone movie magazines, celebrity posters, inexpensive videos, or cassette singles of popular songs.

- Give everyone a copy of their embarrassing Polaroid snapshot.

TROUBLE-SHOOTING TIPS

- If the kids have trouble coming up with acts, prepare some possibilities on slips of paper, put them in a box, and have the kids draw them, one by one—whatever they pick, they must perform.

- Tell the kids not to worry if their act isn't perfect—the more mistakes and flubs, the funnier it will be.

DESIGNER T-SHIRTS

Decorating T-shirts is a wonderful activity for a preteen party—and all of the guests will get to take fun, long-lasting mementos of the party home with them.

For Ages: 10–12

Optional Ages: 6–9

Players Needed: Any group size

Object: To decorate T-shirts with paint

WHAT TO DO

Cover the table with newspapers to prevent a mess and set out all the art materials. Then insert a sheet of cardboard between each T-shirt to make painting easier. It helps to let the kids create designs on paper first, or have a finished T-shirt for them to look at.

The kids can paint the T-shirts using many different techniques. Just read the directions on the paint packages beforehand to know what to do. Another decorating technique, called batik, is also fun. To batik the easy way, buy several packs of crayons, pick out a few primary colors, peel off the wrappers, and break them into pieces. Place the pieces separately in an old muffin tin, along with a piece of paraffin the size of a sugar cube. Hold the muffin tin over a pot of boiling water to

melt the ingredients; then set the tin on a hot plate to keep the crayons melted while the kids use them for painting. When the T-shirts are painted, have the kids crumple them into a ball and dip the entire shirt into a large container of fabric dye. The dye will color the unpainted areas and seep into the cracks created from crumpling the shirts. Remove the shirts from the dye, rinse them thoroughly in cold water, and allow them to air dry until they're just slightly damp. Lay the T-shirts on an ironing board covered with an old towel, and place several paper towels on top of and underneath the painted area of the T-shirts. Iron off the wax by heating the painted area, pulling off the paper towels when soaked, and repeating until the crayon area is soft. Set the finished T-shirts in indirect sunlight or fresh air to dry.

Materials Needed:
- Newspaper
- Cardboard
- Containers for paint
- 1 white T-shirt for each guest
- A variety of T-shirt decorating materials (available at hobby, fabric, and art supply stores)
- Paintbrushes and sponges
- Batik supplies (crayons, paraffin, a muffin tin, a boiling pot, a hot plate, an iron and ironing board, fabric dye, a large container, paintbrushes, an old towel, and paper towels)

CREATIVE OPTIONS

- Rather than painting T-shirts for themselves, the guests can paint special T-shirts for the guest of honor.

- Make simple awards out of construction paper to give to each guest under fun categories like "most colorful," "strangest," or "funniest." Pin the awards to the T-shirts so the kids can wear both home.

- Have the kids make T-shirt designs that go along with the party theme or that are signed by all of the guests—this will help them remember the special day!

PRIZES AND FAVORS

- Send the guests home with their new designer T-shirts.

- Give everyone some T-shirt paints to try the activity again at home.

- Offer the kids T-shirt accessories such as pins or buttons.

TROUBLE-SHOOTING TIPS

- Make one T-shirt ahead of time, using the decorating ideas you plan to try at the party, so that you know how to do the technique. This will help prevent mistakes during the real event.

- The batik process requires adult supervision at all times. Working with hot wax and an iron can be dangerous, so do these steps yourself. If you need help, ask for adult volunteers to come to the party.

SECRET INGREDIENTS

Kids in the kitchen make for a lot of creative fun. Here are the right ingredients for a great time, a good snack, and a grade-A party.

For Ages: 10–12

Optional Ages: 6–9

Players Needed: Any group size

Object: To create delicious treats!

WHAT TO DO

Set the ingredients on the table, and when the kids arrive, divide them into two teams. Tell them they must create an original snack using only the ingredients they find in front of them; then set the timer for fifteen minutes. Let them know their snacks will be judged and that appearance counts as well as taste. Pass out index cards and pens and let the kids give their concoctions a creative name (if there's time, they can decorate the cards, too).

When the time is up, tell the cooks to stop mixing, and have them present their snacks. Pass out paper to all of the guests and have them walk around the table to inspect and taste the snacks. Have them record, out of a possible ten, what each snack is worth in three areas: name, appearance, and taste. Count up

the points and award a prize to the best snack-making team—then let the cooks gobble up the rest of the contest entries!

CREATIVE OPTIONS

- Give each group a different set of ingredients so the snacks will taste different. Be sure to give each group a soft food that will hold the other foods together, and make sure the flavors are compatible.

- Instead of having the cooks judge their own foods, invite a few surprise taste-testers at the end of the cook-off and have them make the final judgement.

- Award prize ribbons for the snacks under categories such as "most original," "most creative," "most unusual," "funniest," "largest," "most like pet food," and so on.

Materials Needed:
- A table
- Food items (peanut butter, yogurt, applesauce, jam, juice, bananas and other fruit, raw vegetables, cheese singles, cereal, crackers, coconut shavings, and chocolate chips)
- Kitchen utensils (spoons, forks, knives, measuring spoons, measuring cups, bowls, plates, cutting boards, mixers, etc.)
- Index cards (3½ by 5½ inches)
- A timer
- Felt-tip pens
- Paper

• Host a "Cook-Off Party"—invite the guests with invitations on recipe cards, and ask the kids to wear aprons or dress like chefs.

PRIZES AND FAVORS

• Send the cooks home with ingredients for chocolate chip cookies and a few samples of the finished product.

• Give the kids samples of the party treats to take home, along with their award ribbons.

• Offer the guests fast food coupons or other food-related gifts.

TROUBLE-SHOOTING TIPS

• Be around to supervise and help, especially if the kids want to use the microwave or other appliances.

• Give the guests special cleanup tasks after the activity—this will make cleaning up easier on everyone, especially you.

PETS ON PARADE

Kids and animals are a winning combination. Take your group of preteen party-goers to a pet show.

For Ages: 10–12

Optional Ages: 6–9

Preparation: Contact a humane society or civic center to find out if any pet shows are scheduled; be sure to ask about times, costs, and directions.

WHAT TO DO

Whether your group is going to a dog, cat, or exotic pets show, the guests will love the experience. Tell the kids ahead of time to bring photos of their pets to show everyone before the outing.

At the show, give the kids ballots (a piece of paper and pencil) so they can vote for the pets they like the best. Have them judge the dogs, cats, or other animals on a variety of serious and silly traits such as best fur color, most fluffy, strangest haircut, best disposition, weirdest-looking, or even most abundant drooler. Also have the kids predict the real winners and award prizes to the kids who guess correctly. Then, for a special treat, give the guests a chance to photograph their favorite animal, using a Polaroid camera. The

kids can share their voting results and snap-shots on the ride home.

CREATIVE OPTIONS

• If going to a pet show is not possible, you can still have a pet-viewing event. Ask the kids to bring their own pets to the party (just be prepared to take care of them!). Or take the kids to a horse show or county/state fair.

• If there's time left after the outing, hold a "barking" or "meowing" contest. Give all the guests a chance to show their stuff—be sure to videotape this, if possible.

• Send the guests invitations written on the back of a photo of the family pet, or on cards shaped liked a dog or cat. Serve hot dogs with "cat-sup," a cake in the shape of a doghouse (call a bakery for details), and let

For Added Fun:
- Paper and pencils for each guest
- A Polaroid camera
- Photos of each guest's pet

the kids eat their meals out of "dog" or "cat" bowls.

PRIZES AND FAVORS

- Send the guests home with squeaky toys for their pets, special pet treats, or, for the kids who don't have pets, stuffed animals.

- Give the guests stickers or posters featuring all sorts of pets.

- Give the winner of the "animal sounds" contest a book about pets or a cartoon book featuring Garfield or Marmaduke.

TROUBLE-SHOOTING TIPS

- Check to see if any of the guests have allergies to fur or specific animals before you plan the event.

- Find adult volunteers to join you on the trip so the kids can walk around freely without getting lost or into trouble.

197

SLUMBER PARTY

Slumber parties are a tradition, and at some point, almost every child wants to have one. Here are some ideas to make your slumber party fun and trouble-free.

For Ages: 10–12

Optional Ages: 6–9

Preparation: Ask the guests to bring their own sleeping bags, but have a few extras on hand in case someone forgets. Plan lots of activities so the kids won't be tempted to play pranks on each other (or on your neighbors!).

WHAT TO DO

When planning a slumber party, it's best to have the guests come during the early evening, rather than the afternoon—the kids will be spending enough time together as it is! If you provide dinner for everyone, have something simple, such as "make-your-own tacos" (this works well for snacking too, which kids love to do at overnighters). Just set the ingredients out in bowls and let the kids prepare their own tacos assembly-line style.

After dinner, play Swami's Secret. Choose one guest to be the Swami and one to be the Swami's Assistant (put a towel "turban" around the Swami's head, for added fun), and secretly tell these guests the trick of the game. The Swami must leave the room so the Assistant can choose another child to be It; then

the Swami returns to amaze everyone by naming that guest. Here's the trick: the Assistant says a sentence beginning with the first letter of It's name when welcoming the Swami back into the room. For example, the Assistant could say, "Just tell us who is It, great Swami," if the person's name is Jennifer. If there are a few guests whose first names begin with the same letter, instruct the Assistant to say a sentence with the first two words beginning with the initials of It's *first* and *last* names. Play until one of the guests figures out the trick.

Later in the evening, let the kids have a good old-fashioned pillow fight. Clear away the furniture and lamps (or send them outside, if the weather permits) and let them pound each other with pillows. Show a movie before bed, if you wish, to help them wind down.

For Added Fun:

- Taco fixings (shells, ground beef, cheddar cheese, tomatoes, lettuce, salsa, sour cream, olives, etc.)
- Bowls
- Lots of pillows
- Extra sleeping bags
- A towel
- *Optional:* a VCR and rented videotape

CREATIVE OPTIONS

- Keep the kids entertained throughout the evening with popular slumber party games, such as Truth or Consequences (see p. 162) or Gossip (see p. 150).

- Provide a cereal buffet in the morning. Just set various kinds of cereal and fruit out, and give each guest a spoon and bowl. All they have to do is add milk—instant breakfast!

- Telling ghost stories is always a popular activity at slumber parties. Turn down the lights and give the storytellers flashlights to shine on their faces as they tell tales.

PRIZES AND FAVORS

- Give the guests Magic Eight Balls (available at toy stores) so they can tell their fortunes all night.

- Offer everyone personalized toothbrushes or pillowcases.

- Send the kids home with boxes of cereal from variety packs, or goody bags filled with cassette singles of popular songs and bubblegum.

TROUBLE-SHOOTING TIPS

- If you rent a scary movie, consider whether the kids will be too scared to sleep.

- Discourage the kids from playing traditional slumber party pranks (such as toilet-papering yards).

BICYCLE RALLY

Combining fun with adventure makes for a great party outing. This bicycle trip has lots of surprises to keep the riders moving along, while providing good exercise.

For Ages: 10–12

Optional Ages: 6–9

Preparation: Make sure the guests have bicycles that are in good working order and that they wear helmets. Scout and map out a safe route for a group of bicycling kids.

WHAT TO DO

Once you choose the route for the party, travel it once on your own bike and make notes about the length of the course, turns, landmarks, and other points of interest along the way. Look for places to securely hang paper plates.

On the day of the party, write up some directions on each paper plate that will help the cyclists find their way to the end of the course. For example, on one paper plate you might instruct the riders to turn at a fork in the road—if they miss the turn, they'll end up going out of their way (hang plates that say, "Oops, go back," in case this happens). You can make the clues simple or complex, depending on how long you want the bike rally to last. Then mount the plates (using a staple gun, tacks, or tape) to the landmarks you've chosen, having them all point to a fun destination, such as a restaurant or picnic area. Always make sure the plates are at eye level so the kids won't miss them, and be sure that the plates won't be defacing property.

For added fun, write up some riddles or trivia questions on each paper plate for the kids to solve and answer. Tell them to secretly write their answers on paper—but be sure they understand that they can confer with other cyclists on the course directions. Gather the "bikers" together and tell them the rules of the bike rally. Then watch them go! If their destination is a picnic area, plan for another adult to welcome them with a picnic lunch you've packed ahead of time. Or, enjoy lunch at a restaurant.

For Added Fun:
- Paper plates
- Felt-tip pens
- Paper and a pencil or pen for each rider
- A staple gun, tacks, or heavy tape

CREATIVE OPTIONS

- Instead of using paper plates to mark the route, give each cyclist a map of the course. Make it more challenging to follow by omitting street names and using directions such as "Turn left at first chance." Mark the map with landmarks so they won't get lost.

- If it's not possible to have the cyclists end up at a restaurant, take them on a circuitous route that leads them right back to your home. While they're biking, arrange for another adult to set up the party room with "Welcome Home" balloons, a fun meal, and plenty of cold drinks.

PRIZES AND FAVORS

- Give the guests small, personalized bicycle license plates with their first names on them (available at bike shops or toy stores).

- Give them all T-shirts to wear on the rally, with the inscription: "I Survived the Bike Party!"

TROUBLE-SHOOTING TIPS

- Check the kids' bikes to make sure they're in good working order before the trip. (Bring along a patch kit and tire pump, in case there's trouble.)

- Find some adult volunteers to help keep everyone on track and safe. For a longer distance, follow along in a car or other vehicle to rescue any bikers who get a flat.

- Be sure to go over the rules of the road before the trip begins. Bike safety is very important, even on secluded roads.

PAJAMA BREAKFAST

Wake up—it's time to party! This surprise pajama breakfast is a hoot—for the hosts, the guests, and anyone else who's lucky enough to share in the fun.

For Ages: 10–12

Optional Ages: 6–9

Preparation: Make reservations at a restaurant that specializes in breakfast food, and tell them about your party plans (make sure they don't have a "No-Pajamas" dress code!). Let the parents know about the surprise, but don't tell the guests.

WHAT TO DO

After you've warned the restaurant staff of your plans, call the guests' parents and explain the details of the event. Tell them not to inform the kids of the plan, but to make sure they wear decent pajamas the night before.

Early on the morning of the party (six or seven a.m.), awaken the guest of honor, hop in the car, and collect the party guests, one by one. At each house, have the guest of honor go up to the door to alert the parent that it's time for the party, then awaken the sleeping guest. Make sure the guests wear only their pajamas, robes, and slippers or tennis shoes and socks (no changing clothes unless they're absolutely *not* decent).

As the party crowd gets larger, let them all awaken and greet the other snoozing guests.

Once you have everyone, head for the next surprise—breakfast at a restaurant! The event is silly and only slightly embarrassing, and it's lots of fun for the guests to enter the restaurant in their pajamas. Let the guests order whatever they want, enjoy the scene they're making, and return home to begin the rest of their day.

CREATIVE OPTIONS

- If you'd prefer not to go out in public, you can kidnap the "sleeping beauties" for a breakfast buffet at your home.

- Coordinate with the other parents to hold a "progressive" breakfast party. After gathering all of the guests, drive the route again, this time stopping at each home for a part of the breakfast meal—go to one house for juice; one for fruit; one for cereal; one for

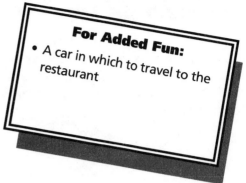

For Added Fun:
• A car in which to travel to the restaurant

pancakes, eggs, and bacon; and one for cake or dessert. Then drop off the satisfied guests at their own homes again.

• Host an overnight party and wake the kids early for the surprise pajama breakfast.

PRIZES AND FAVORS

• Give the pajama-wearing gang some hair accessories to manage their "morning hair."

• Give everyone inexpensive slippers, fun toothbrushes, and bubblegum-flavored toothpaste.

• Hand out mini boxes of cereal from variety packs.

TROUBLE-SHOOTING TIPS

• Be sure the guests are wearing pajamas, a robe, and slippers so they won't be too embarrassed—restaurants require footwear of some kind, so slippers or tennis shoes are a must.

• Be sure to prepare the restaurant staff for your visit, to avoid any problems. Ask if they have a banquet room available to ensure privacy and to keep the noise level down.

• Tell the guest of honor to wake the guests gently, allowing them to brush their teeth and hair—you don't want any crabby, messy guests!

DAY AT THE BEACH

Any ocean, lake, river, or pool will make a perfect setting for a beach party. Just gather the kids, add water and sunshine, and serve up a great time!

For Ages: 10–12

Optional Ages: 6–9

Preparation: Find an ocean, lake, river, or pool for the party. Recruit some adults or older teen volunteers to act as lifeguards.

WHAT TO DO

Plan the beach party during a sunny season (but have an alternative plan, in case Mother Nature is having a bad day). Specify on the invitations that the guests bring their bathing suits and towels to the party. Then hop in the car and head to the beach.

When you arrive, organize some group beach games such as volleyball, Frisbee, and jai alai (for jai alai, rinse and clean bleach bottles thoroughly and cut them into scoops, leaving the handles intact—have the kids stand in a circle and toss a small ball to one another using the scoops to catch and throw). When the kids are ready to get wet, break for a swim or a squirt gun fight.

While the kids are swimming, get the hibachi going and cook hot dogs, burgers, or s'mores.

When everyone runs out of energy, hold a sand-sculpting competition. Divide the kids into teams and have them make super sand castles and sculptures—they can use the jai alai scoops as tools. Spend about two hours in the sun; then shake off the sand, collect the gear, and wave good-bye to the beach.

CREATIVE OPTIONS

- Instead of having organized games, just provide the guests with rafts or other flotation devices and let them ride the waves and soak up the sun.

- If the weather turns bad, have a beach party anyway—even at home! Ask the guests to wear their bathing suits, and spend the day watching a beach movie, eating party food, and listening or dancing to music.

For Added Fun:
- A Frisbee
- A volleyball and net
- Beach balls
- 1 large, empty bleach bottle per guest
- Squirt guns
- Small balls for everyone
- A hibachi or grill, with plenty of food to cook

- Invite the guests to the party by sending inexpensive sunglasses or beach balls with the party information attached. Or send the guests postcards featuring the ocean; tuck them into envelopes with the party details, add a little sand, and mail.

PRIZES AND FAVORS

- Send the kids home with beach toys—jai alai scoops, squirt guns, or Frisbees.

- Give everyone a pair of sunglasses and some sunscreen.

- Offer beach towels or T-shirt cover-ups.

- Give everyone a beach ball to use during the event or to take home.

TROUBLE-SHOOTING TIPS

- Make sure the kids wear shoes to the beach, in case the sand is hot or there is broken glass or litter around.

- Provide sunscreen for all of the guests and encourage them to apply it frequently.

- Adult supervision is vital for all swimming activities. If you have a large group, make sure you have more than one lifeguard.

FABULOUS FORTUNE-TELLER

There's something fabulous and fascinating about fortune-tellers (even if they can't predict so much as the weather!). You can "predict" a fun event when you invite a fortune-teller to your party.

For Ages: 10–12

Optional Ages: 6–9

Preparation: Find a professional fortune-teller by looking in the Yellow Pages under "Entertainers." For a less-expensive alternative, arrange for a friend or family member to do the job (clothing and make-up are available at costume shops).

WHAT TO DO

You can find a fortune-teller through a special company or agency, or you can hire one that works independently. Interview several by phone ahead of time to determine which performance or act is right for your party and guests. Some fortune-tellers tell fortunes with crystal balls or cards, some read palms, and some even read tea leaves! Prepare some fun predictions on paper for the guests ahead of time, such as who the guests will marry (name some teenage heartthrobs), where they'll live (a shack or a mansion), what careers they'll have (grave digger or movie star), what kind of car they'll drive (an old school bus or a limousine), and other fun fortunes.

For extra fun, work with the fortune-teller to set up some predictions that actually come true during the party—thanks to some sneaky planning ahead of time. You might predict that a guest's mother will call at a certain time (and she does!—with an arrangement beforehand), that a certain song will come on the radio at a certain time (tape record a station ahead of time and play it during the party), and that someone at the party will spill or drop something (it's bound to happen!).

CREATIVE OPTIONS

• Create some fun horoscopes to give to the guests to read aloud (find out their birthdates before the party), and let them play with a Ouija board.

• Make the atmosphere of the party mysterious—place dry ice around the "crystal ball," lay out some tarot cards, and hang

For Added Fun:
- Paper and a pencil or pen
- A cassette player
- Blank cassette tapes for pre-recording songs

astrological charts on the wall; then play spooky music, dim the lights, and light some candles.

- Serve fortune cookies to the guests. You can fill them with fun fortunes that you create yourself. Just type up some witty or silly predictions, cut them into small strips, pull out the original fortunes with tweezers, and insert your own (personalize them as much as possible).

PRIZES AND FAVORS

- Give the guests their own Magic Eight Balls, an astrology chart, a book of horoscopes, or other fortune-telling items.

- Send the kids home with their fortune cookies and fortunes.

- Take Polaroid snapshots of the guests with the fortune-teller to give away.

TROUBLE-SHOOTING TIP

- When choosing a fortune-teller, make sure you choose one who will be compatible with the fun spirit of a kids' party. Explain that the fortunes can't be too serious or scary in any way—especially if the medium is doing a tarot card reading.

BAKE ME A CAKE

A decorated cake is a special part of every party, and it's extra special if the kids can do the decorating themselves. Here's a party that really takes the cake!

For Ages: 10–12

Optional Ages: 6–9

Preparation: Contact a bakery to find a cake-decorating expert. For a less-expensive alternative, make arrangements with a friend or family member who is an expert in the decorating craft.

WHAT TO DO

When looking for a cake decorator, try to find one who is accustomed to teaching and working with kids. Request that the cake decorator bring samples of his or her work, and be sure you know ahead of time what type of decorating materials you'll need on hand (the decorator might provide supplies, too). Specify on the invitations that the kids wear clothes that can get a little messy or that they bring smocks or old shirts.

Depending on the decorator you hire, he or she might bring a cake that all of the kids can work on, and show them how to make frosted flowers, leaves, and other fun decorations. If you wish, you can also prepare cupcakes or a couple of large sheet cakes (cut into squares) for the kids to decorate—freeze the cakes

ahead of time to make it easier to spread the frosting. Tint the cake frosting a variety of colors, using food coloring, and set out the decorating items on a table for easy access. Take pictures of the frosted cakes before the kids gobble them up!

CREATIVE OPTIONS

- If you decide to use sheet cake squares, let the kids decorate the squares individually; then put them back together to form one large "patchwork" cake.

- For simpler cake decorating, buy an easy-to-operate decorating kit from a grocery store. Then just twist on a decorating tip and squeeze out the pre-made frosting.

- Invite the guests by hand-delivering a large cookie with the party details written in

For Added Fun:
- Cakes or cupcakes to decorate
- Cake-decorating tubes, papers, and accessories
- Ready-made frosting or frosting ingredients
- Food coloring
- A variety of cake decorations
- A camera or videocamera to take pictures

frosting. Or send them a "recipe for party fun" with the party details written like a recipe card.

PRIZES AND FAVORS

- Send the guests home with any extra cakes or cupcakes.

- Give everyone a box of cake mix, a tube of frosting with a decorator tip attached, and some sugar decorations.

- Give each child an apron and chef's hat to take home (available at department stores).

TROUBLE-SHOOTING TIPS

- Be sure the kids wash their hands before handling the food.

- Tell the kids to wear old clothes to the party, if you're worried about chocolate or other food stains.

- Remind the kids to be courteous when waiting their turn to decorate.

DANCING WITH A DJ

Kids love to dance, so why not host a dancing party complete with a disc jockey playing popular tunes? Have your guest of honor help choose the type of music, then clear the dance floor and let the kids dance all night.

For Ages: 10–12

Optional Ages: 6–9

Preparation: Find a professional disc jockey by looking in the Yellow Pages under "Disc Jockeys." For a less-expensive alternative, arrange for a family member or teen to do the job. The guests can bring their own musical selections, too.

WHAT TO DO

When hiring a disc jockey, shop around, because fees vary. You can have the disc jockey bring music or you can provide your own. Hire a disc jockey who is accustomed to working with kids and who can help "break the ice" at the beginning of the party.

Ask the guests to wear their dancing clothes—they can go fancy or trendy, as long as they can move around in what they're wearing! Then decorate the party room with posters of rock groups and singers, hang a strobe light or Christmas lights for atmosphere (dim the overhead lights), and, for extra fun, rent a bubble machine. Once the stage is set, let the kids dance to their hearts' content.

For added fun, have a lip-sync contest before the dancing begins (have the kids volunteer

for this). Just play a popular song and let the kids show off their "musical skill" for a few minutes. This will help everyone get in the mood for dancing and fun.

CREATIVE OPTIONS

• Hold a dance contest with you or the disc jockey as the judge.

• Find a volunteer (a friend, family member, or neighborhood teen) to teach the kids some fun new or old dances.

• Videotape the kids dancing, then play the tape later for fun. Pretend you're taping a televised dance show (such as "American Bandstand") and "interview" the kids about the music, their favorite singers, and their special requests.

• Take Polaroid snapshots of the kids dancing to hand out as favors later.

For Added Fun:

- A big room with a floor fit for dancing
- Posters of rock groups or singers
- A strobe light or Christmas lights
- *Optional:* a bubble machine

- Provide party food and drinks while the disc jockey takes a break.

PRIZES AND FAVORS

- Give everyone a cassette single of a popular song.

- Send dance contest winners home with a rock group poster, record, or CD.

- Give everyone inexpensive items with a musical theme—key chains shaped like musical notes, buttons featuring singers, or pins shaped like guitars.

TROUBLE-SHOOTING TIPS

- Move furniture and breakables out of the way to prevent any accidents.

- Make sure the disc jockey's sound system is compatible with the amount of space you have in the party room.

- Don't force the guests to pair off into couples at mixer parties—depending on the age and maturity level of the group, they might be shy about boy/girl dancing.

- Have the disc jockey play slow songs regularly, so the kids don't get too worn out.

Order Form

Qty.	Title	Author	Order No.	Unit Cost (U.S. $)	Total
	Bad Case of the Giggles	Lansky, B.	2411	$15.00	
	Best Baby Shower Book	Cooke, C.	1239	$7.00	
	Best Baby Shower Party Game Book	Cooke, C.	6063	$3.95	
	Best Birthday Party Game Book	Lansky, B.	6064	$3.95	
	Best Bridal Shower Game Book	Cooke, C.	6060	$3.95	
	Best Couple's Shower Party Game Book	Cooke, C.	6061	$3.95	
	Best Party Book	Warner, P.	6089	$8.00	
	Best Wedding Shower Book	Cooke, C.	6059	$7.00	
	Free Stuff for Kids	Free Stuff Editors	2190	$5.00	
	Games People Play	Warner, P.	6093	$8.00	
	Girls to the Rescue	Lansky, B.	2215	$3.95	
	Just for Fun Party Game Book	Warner, P.	6065	$3.95	
	Kids Are Cookin'	Brown, K.	2440	$8.00	
	Kids' Holiday Fun	Warner, P.	6000	$12.00	
	Kids' Party Cookbook	Warner, P.	2435	$12.00	
	Kids' Party Games and Activities	Warner, P.	6095	$12.00	
	Kids' Pick-A-Party Book	Warner, P.	6090	$9.00	
	Kids Pick the Funniest Poems	Lansky, B.	2410	$15.00	
	Over-the-Hill Party Game Book	Cooke, C.	6062	$3.95	
	Pick A Party	Sachs, P.	6085	$9.00	
	Poetry Party	Lansky, B.	2430	$12.00	
				Subtotal	
				Shipping and Handling (see below)	
				MN residents add 6.5% sales tax	
				Total	

YES! Please send me the books indicated above. Add $2.00 shipping and handling for the first book and 50¢ for each additional book. Add $2.50 to total for books shipped to Canada. Overseas postage will be billed. Allow up to four weeks for delivery. Send check or money order payable to Meadowbrook Press. No cash or C.O.D.'s, please. Prices subject to change without notice. **Quantity discounts available upon request.**

Send book(s) to:

Name _____ Address _____

City _____ State _____ Zip _____

Telephone (_____)_____ P.O. number (if necessary) _____

Payment via:

❑ Check or money order payable to Meadowbrook Press (No cash or C.O.D.'s, please)   Amount enclosed $ _____

❑ Visa (for orders over $10.00 only)   ❑ MasterCard (for orders over $10.00 only)

Account # _____ Signature _____ Exp. Date _____

A *FREE* Meadowbrook Press catalog is available upon request.

You can also phone us for orders of $10.00 or more at **1-800-338-2232.**

Mail to: Meadowbrook Press
5451 Smetana Drive, Minnetonka, MN 55343
Toll-Free 1-800-338-2232

Phone (612) 930-1100

Fax (612) 930-1940